AMSTERDAM
ENCOUNTER

ZORA O'NEILL

Amsterdam Encounter

Published by Lonely Planet Publications Pty Ltd
ABN 36 005 607 983

Australia	Head Office, Locked Bag 1, Footscray, Victoria 3011 ☎ 03 8379 8000 fax 03 8379 8111 talk2us@lonelyplanet.com.au
USA	150 Linden St, Oakland, CA 94607 ☎ 510 250 6400 toll free 800 275 8555 fax 510 893 8572 info@lonelyplanet.com
UK	2nd fl, 186 City Rd, London EC1V 2NT ☎ 020 7106 2100 fax 020 7106 2101 go@lonelyplanet.co.uk

This title was commissioned in Lonely Planet's London office and produced by: **Commissioning Editors** Lucy Monie, Jo Potts **Coordinating Editor** Barbara Delissen **Coordinating Cartographer** Brendan Streager **Layout Designer** Carlos Solarte **Managing Editor** Imogen Bannister **Managing Cartographer** Alison Lyall **Managing Layout Designer** Celia Wood **Assisting Editors** Chris Girdler, Anne Mulvaney, Erin Richards **Cover Researcher** Naomi Parker, lonelyplanetimages.com **Project Manager** Annelies Mertens **Thanks to** Melanie Dankel, Craig Kilburn, Indra Kilfoyle, Lisa Knights, Lyahna Spencer, Glenn Vanderknijff, Aude Vauconsant, Gerard Walker

ISBN 978 1 74179 706 0

Printed by Hang Tai Printing Company, Hong Kong
Printed in China

Acknowledgement Amsterdam Transport Network Map © GVB Amsterdam.

MIX
Paper from
responsible sources
FSC™ C021741
www.fsc.org

HOW TO USE THIS BOOK
Colour-Coding & Maps
Colour-coding is used for symbols on maps and in the text that they relate to (eg all eating venues on the maps and in the text are given a green knife and fork symbol). Each neighbourhood also gets its own colour, and this is used down the edge of the page and throughout that neighbourhood section.

Shaded yellow areas on the maps denote 'areas of interest' – for their historical significance, their attractive architecture or their great bars and restaurants. We encourage you to head to these areas and just start exploring!

Prices
Multiple prices listed with reviews (eg €10/5 or €10/5/20) indicate adult/child, adult/concession or adult/child/family.

Send us your feedback We love to hear from readers – your comments help make our books better. We read every word you send us, and we always guarantee that your feedback goes straight to the appropriate authors. The most useful submissions are rewarded with a free book. To send us your updates and find out about Lonely Planet events, newsletters and travel news visit our award-winning website: *lonelyplanet.com/contact*.

Note: We may edit, reproduce and incorporate your comments in Lonely Planet products such as guidebooks, websites and digital products, so let us know if you don't want your comments reproduced or your name acknowledged. For a copy of our privacy policy visit *lonelyplanet.com/privacy*.

ZORA O'NEILL

Fresh out of college, Zora O'Neill arrived in Amsterdam to work at a cafe adjoining a scrappy improv theatre (now the comedy juggernaut Boom Chicago; p93). Her job description called for dispensing tourist advice along with grilled sandwiches – a bit flawed, considering she'd just arrived herself. If you got lost looking for that 'super easy-to-find' bike route to Marken in 1994, Zora's very sorry. Fortunately, she's much more qualified now; with in-laws, friends and her own bike in Amsterdam, she visits every year. The first thing she does when she arrives is eat a *broodje haring* (p89), and the second thing she does is get on a boat. The rest of the year, she lives in Astoria, Queens, where she writes about food and travel. Zora has been a guidebook author since 2003; this is her fourth book for Lonely Planet.

ZORA'S THANKS

Many thanks to Rod Ben Zeev, Ingalil Hubert, Klary Koopmans, Mark Morse, Andrew Moskos and Edwin Oppedijk, plus a special shoutout to Mike LoBianco, Chirag Patel and fickle Eyjafjallajökull. My interviewees gave me new insights (and oysters!), and Peter, as ever, steered the boat. At Lonely Planet, thanks to Lucy Monie.

Our readers Many thanks to the travellers who wrote to us with helpful hints, useful advice and interesting anecdotes: Xenia Aidonopoulou, Alice Barley, Jeroen Komen, Conor Leahy, Simon Pollentine, Nils Rondhuis, Sandra Salomonsson, Kerren Schooneman.

Cover photograph Bicycles parked by Singel canal. Amsterdam, North Holland, Netherlands, Europe; Frans Lemmens/LPI

Internal photographs p21 Dennis Cox/Alamy; p131 Arco Images GmbH/Alamy; p15 (Rag chair for Droog by Tejo Remy) Robaard/Theuwkens; p24 Netherlands Board of Tourism & Conventions; p156 Eduard Bergman (NBTC); p49, p71, p87, p107 by Zora O'Neill. All other photographs by Lonely Planet Images, and by Will Salter except p8 Christian Aslund; p4 Paul Beinssen; p28 Simon Foale; p159 Amerens Hedwich; p22, p40, p52, p64, p76, p94, p98, p116, p118, p141, p142 Martin Moos; p11, p165 Richard Nebesky; p36 Zaw Min Yu.

All images are copyright of the photographers unless otherwise indicated. Many of the images in this guide are available for licensing from **Lonely Planet Images**: www.lonelyplanetimages.com.

On your bike: take to the streets on two wheels, in one of the world's most cycle-friendly cities

CONTENTS

Why is our travel information the best in the world? It's simple: our authors are passionate, dedicated travellers. They don't take freebies in exchange for positive coverage so you can be sure the advice you're given is impartial. They travel widely to all the popular spots, and off the beaten track. They don't research using just the internet or phone. They discover new places not included in any other guidebook. They personally visit thousands of hotels, restaurants, palaces, trails, galleries, temples and more. They speak with dozens of locals every day to make sure you get the kind of insider knowledge only a local could tell you. They take pride in getting all the details right, and in telling it how it is. Think you can do it? Find out how at **lonelyplanet.com**.

THIS IS AMSTERDAM

You're sitting on a small boat, sliding along the curve of the Prinsengracht. It's twilight, and the sky is painted the richest indigo. The white lights edging the canal bridges reflect on the black water, and the windows in the gabled houses glow gold.

It's just another gorgeous evening in Amsterdam, a magical city where 17th-century buildings lean against each other like fond old friends, and the mindset of residents is one of the most progressive in the world.

Amsterdam may be famous for its pragmatic approach to sex and drugs, but once you're here for more than an afternoon, you'll see how this policy fits right into a city that values its inhabitants' rights to pursue their interests – whether that means opening a shop specialising in toothbrushes or skating around town in nothing but a rhinestone-studded jockstrap.

It is true that Amsterdammers will take any excuse to party till dawn, and concert halls and clubs are booked solid with entertainment from all over the globe. Combine this with a flourishing design scene and catwalk style during the biannual fashion week, and it's hard to believe that Amsterdam is a city of only 750,000 people.

It is growing though, as you'll see from the construction scaffolding visible all over town. With a new metro line being laid and a harbour that seems to sprout a fresh architectural marvel every month, this metropolis is in fast-forward motion. In recent years, debates over immigration, right-leaning national politics and a global economic meltdown have caused citywide anxiety. But Amsterdammers are too relaxed to live in crisis mode. They've gotten back to business, settled into their beloved candle-lit bars, flocked to the clubs – or donned their wigs and platform boots and hopped back on their bicycles. In short, they're still doing their own thing. Care to join in? Just pack a few days' attitude, and climb aboard.

Top left Getting into the swing of things at the Dampkring coffeeshop (p53) **Top right** The sun sets on Groenburgwal canal in the heart of the Southern Canal Belt **Bottom** A motorcyclist pauses outside Koninklijk Paleis (p42)

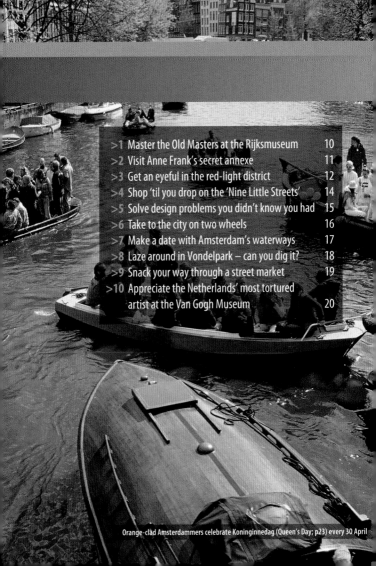

Orange-clad Amsterdammers celebrate Koninginnedag (Queen's Day; p23) every 30 April

>1 RIJKSMUSEUM

MASTER THE OLD MASTERS AT THE RIJKSMUSEUM

The Rijksmuseum (p98) is the Netherlands' treasure house, established when the country was one of the wealthiest in the world. It has grown into a collection of more than a million objects of art, including 5000 paintings, which represent the artists of the Dutch Golden Age as well as notable works from elsewhere in Europe. Pending completion of the monumental 1885 building's renovation in 2013, currently only a small portion of the treasures are on view in a side wing. Hardcore art-lovers will be a bit disappointed, but in many ways this limited selection, which takes about two hours to see, is a very manageable treat.

All the greatest hits are here, including portraits by Frans Hals, rowdy pub scenes by Jan Steen, domestic tableaux by Johannes Vermeer and the glowing cows that Paulus Potter specialised in. If you're lucky, you'll also see Jan Asselijn's malevolent swan – but the exact selections, which might also include examples of fine delftware and some of the 17th- and 18th-century dollhouses the museum owns, change a few times a year. One work, though, is always on display – Rembrandt's *The Night Watch,* a strikingly luminous work that broke new ground in the field of civic guards' portraits.

>2 ANNE FRANK HUIS
VISIT ANNE FRANK'S SECRET ANNEXE

Young Anne Frank would have been another anonymous victim of the Holocaust were it not for her illuminating diary, written during the two years she and her family lived hidden in the back of her father's offices with another family attempting to avoid Nazi persecution. Translated into some 60 languages and adapted as a stage play and film, her writing reflects all the travails of an ordinary teenage girl, unable to swim against the tide of extraordinary times. The hidden families were eventually revealed to the Gestapo, and Anne died in Bergen-Belsen concentration camp just months before the war ended.

The focus of Anne Frank Huis (p62) is the *achterhuis* (rear house), the secret annexe behind a revolving bookcase. It was in this dark and airless space that the Franks observed complete silence during the day, outgrew their clothes, pasted photos of Hollywood stars on the walls and read Dickens, before being mysteriously betrayed and sent to their deaths. The claustrophobic rooms, their windows still covered with blackout screens, are bare of furniture at the request of Anne's father Otto, the only member of the group to survive the camps. But poignant traces are still visible – the children's heights marked on the door frame, for instance. The house has been a museum since 1957, and now incorporates a modern wing that addresses issues of present-day racism and anti-Semitism.

>3 DE WALLEN

GET AN EYEFUL IN THE RED-LIGHT DISTRICT

As much as the tourism board wishes it weren't so, the district called De Wallen (The Quays) is a distinguishing feature of Amsterdam. Perhaps what's most fascinating about the red-light district is that it's not a festering den of sleaze. Granted, lads on lost weekends don't set a great tone, but this may be the safest vice zone in the world. De Wallen is a functioning neighbourhood, complete with kids, older residents, cosy cafes and postcard-worthy canals.

To the Dutch, legal prostitution is simply common sense, as is, for that matter, the marijuana sold at the 'coffeeshops' that alternate with the pubs, sex shops and peep-show theatres. But it's still mind-bending when you first set eyes on the women in the windows, illuminated not only with red lights, but also with black ones that make their white lingerie glow enticingly. (Your first instinct might be to take a photo, but don't do it – out of simple respect, and to avoid having your camera tossed in a canal by the ladies' enforcers.)

Go first in the midmorning, when the neighbourhood is waking up: prostitutes on the early shift chat out their windows as grannies go out for a stroll. Stop in at De Bakkerswinkel (p47) or Hofje van Wijs (p48) for a pastry and a *koffie verkeerd* (milky coffee), and visit the beautiful Oude Kerk (p43), the city's oldest house of worship. Take a tour at the Prostitution Information Centre (p43), and finish with a shot of *jenever* (Dutch-style gin) at Wynand Fockink (p56).

Come back in the evening, when all the neon lights are on, and

---

RED MEANS STOP?

In early 2008 the city government announced it wanted to 'restore the balance' in De Wallen, citing too much influence of organised crime in prostitution and coffeeshops. To encourage entrepreneurs to invest in cleaner businesses in the area, the city is acting as a guarantor for investors to buy brothel buildings. Firm plans for the properties are still being worked out – 'but it won't involve McDonald's or Starbucks', one city official assured us. Visitors probably won't see the effects of the project for several years, but it shouldn't mean the end of the red-light windows altogether.

edge down the city's narrowest alley, the metre-wide Trompetter-steeg, lined with red-light windows (look for the entrance in the block south of the Oude Kerk). Maybe take in a live sex show at Casa Rosso (p57), or just head to one of the many nonexplicit nightspots, like Winston Kingdom (p57) or In 't Aepjen (p55).

It's worth noting that this isn't the only red-light district in Amsterdam – there's another stretch of windows on Spuistraat, and some on Ruysdaelkade in De Pijp. Likewise, there are coffeeshops all over the city as well (see p161). But nowhere else has quite the stimulating mix of history and industry as De Wallen.

>4 NEGEN STRAATJES

SHOP 'TIL YOU DROP ON THE 'NINE LITTLE STREETS'

In a city packed with shopping opportunities, the Negen Straatjes represent the very densest concentration of consumer pleasures. These nine streets are indeed quite small, each one a block long. They form a grid connecting the three main canals in the Western Canal Belt, south of Raadhuisstraat. The shops here are also quite small, and many are highly specialised. For velvet ribbons, visit HJ van de Kerkhof (p66); for toothbrushes, De Witte Tanden Winkel (p65); for single-edition art books, Boekie Woekie (p64). It's also the place to head for fashion: edgy Belgian and Dutch designers at Van Ravenstein (p68), eye-popping shoes at Hester van Eeghen (p66) or vintage treasures at Laura Dols (p67). This book would sink under the weight of all the delightful shops, so we've included only a handful and left the rest for you to discover (extra points if you find the doll doctor!).

After zigzagging through even a portion of the streets, you'll probably need some rejuvenation – no problem, because there are plenty of cafes in the Negen Straatjes as well. Tuck into a sandwich at Buffet van Odette (p68), or enjoy the peace and quiet at De Pels (p74). Note that shopkeepers in the Negen Straatjes like to relax too – many are closed entirely on Monday, and sometimes Tuesday, so plan your grand tour for later in the week.

>5 DUTCH DESIGN

SOLVE DESIGN PROBLEMS YOU DIDN'T KNOW YOU HAD

Built on piles sunk deep in a bog and cut through with serene canals, the whole city of Amsterdam is an elegant design solution. So it's no surprise that Dutch design has a reputation for creative approaches to everyday objects. A few big names – Hella Jongerius, Gijs Bakker and Marcel Wanders – are known internationally, but true to inclusive Amsterdam form, the best work often comes out of collectives such as Droog (p126), where member designers needn't be Dutch – they just need to think as if they are, and have a knack for repurposing, reinventing and sometimes just laughing. Droog's signature designs employ surreal humour (a chandelier made of 80-plus light bulbs clustered like fish eggs) as well as practicality, as in the off-centre umbrella, surely inspired by the country's weather.

Dutch designers take a cock-eyed look at their own heritage too. At Amsterdam's temple of home decor, Frozen Fountain (p65), you can see tongue-in-cheek versions of delftware and traditional textiles. But gems from the past are treasured at Bebob Design (p85), Wonderwood (p47) and other vintage specialists.

The stereotypically thrifty Dutch love a well-designed bargain too. All-purpose shop HEMA (p45) has developed a cult following by commissioning design students to put a spin on everything from espresso cups to handbags. Once you have a hand towel with a rivet in one corner for hanging, you'll wonder how you lived without it!

>6 BICYCLES

TAKE TO THE CITY ON TWO WHEELS

With the possible exception of Copenhagen, no other city in the world is quite as bicycle-mad as Amsterdam. Dutch riders see their two-wheeled transport as nothing special, but one of the greatest sights for visitors is the sheer diversity of the city's bicycles. Among the estimated 600,000 bikes in the city, you'll spot everything from the standard curvy black *omafiets* (granny bike) to flashy customised jobs trimmed with plastic flowers. Mums load toddlers in the front bins of their *bakfietsen* (cargo bikes) or stack the kids on front and back seats. Hip youngsters in teensy skirts arrive at nightclubs on bikes, and bankers zip off to work on theirs, ties flapping in the breeze.

By far the best way to appreciate Amsterdam's bicycle-friendliness is to ride one yourself. They're available for rent all over (see p175 for a couple of recommended companies), and once you're up and rolling, you'll see the city from a whole new angle, shoulder to shoulder with local commuters on the 400km of dedicated cycle paths. It's worth devoting a day to near-aimless cycling – pick one relatively distant sight, like the Tropenmuseum (p113) or the cool architecture of the Eastern Docklands (p132), and let yourself get lost on your way there. Once you have a taste of the freedom a bike affords, you won't want to give it up.

>7 CANALS
MAKE A DATE WITH AMSTERDAM'S WATERWAYS

To say Amsterdammers love the water is an understatement. Sure, the city made its first fortune in maritime trade, but that's ancient history. Here in the present, on a sunny Sunday afternoon, you can see the local aquaphilia just by sitting canalside and watching the boats go by. Some cafes – such as Spanjer en van Twist (p72) and 't Smalle (p77) – seem purpose-built for this sport. Or you could stroll next to the canals and check out some of the city's 3300 houseboats. The Prinsengracht is lined with a particularly great mix of homes, from mod blocks to cobbled-together creations, and you can even tour one at the Houseboat Museum (p62).

Definitely make time in your schedule for a canal tour (p178). If it's raining, you'll have to take one of the giant glassed-in boats, but if it's clear, hop aboard a smaller open-air operation and feel the wind in your hair. A short (and free) ferry ride (p175) across the IJ harbour gives you a taste of the industrial side of Amsterdam's watery heritage – and if you like that, you can dine on a boat as well (p51).

From boat level you'll get to see a whole new set of architectural details, like the ornamentation on all the bridges. And when you pass the canalside cafe terraces, you can just look up and wave.

>8 VONDELPARK

LAZE AROUND IN VONDELPARK – CAN YOU DIG IT?

As integral to Amsterdam as the canals and cafes, Vondelpark (p99) is the place to be on a sunny day. The long, narrow park was laid out as a green belt for the Amsterdam elite in the 1860s, and named after the poet and playwright Joost van den Vondel (the Shakespeare of the Dutch language). But the rambling green space has been thoroughly democratised since then, thanks in part to the hippies who camped here en masse in the summer of 1970.

As representatives of every thread of Amsterdam's social fabric descend, a party atmosphere ensues. Some people kick back by reading a book, some cradle a beer at one of the cafes, some share a spliff and strum songs on the guitar. Street performers work the crowds and kids rush the playgrounds. The atmosphere is so anything-goes, in fact, that the city council debated legalising anonymous sex in the infamous cruising grounds of the rose gardens. The law didn't pass – so now the scene is, like so many things here, simply 'tolerated'. Oddly, though, topless sunbathing is technically banned. But plenty of women still strip off their tops to work on their tans. Ponds, lawns and winding footpaths encourage visitors to explore. Keep your eyes and ears open – you might hear an organ concert or see a flock of parakeets.

>9 ALBERT CUYPMARKT

SNACK YOUR WAY THROUGH A STREET MARKET

You *could* go to the half-mile-long Albert Cuypmarkt (p106) to buy pink plastic sandals, a whole fish, a bike lock or cheap lingerie. You could also go to marvel at Amsterdam in all its diversity, as the century-old market is in the middle of a neighbourhood known for its immigrant roots. Stalls cater to Surinamese, Moroccan and Indonesian clientele, and to cheese-lovers wherever they may hail from. Vendors loudly tout their odd gadgets and their stupendous arrays of fresh fruit.

But we wouldn't want you to get distracted by the scene and overlook the snacks. Certainly you can get *frites* (French or, more correctly, Belgian fries) from a few stands along the route, but you can also savour some other essential culinary titbits the Dutch hold dear. Start your lunch with a *broodje haring* – raw herring on a soft bun, topped with sweet pickles (for more on this treat, see the boxed text on p89). Then tuck into a fresh-fried *loempia,* a crispy miniature egg roll that entered Dutch culinary tradition via Indonesia – make sure you don't forget the sweet-hot sauce. For dessert, track down the *stroopwafel* man, who doles out thin cookies stuck together with caramel, hot off a dedicated griddle. You can smell the cinnamon from a block away.

>10 VAN GOGH MUSEUM

APPRECIATE THE NETHERLANDS' MOST TORTURED ARTIST AT THE VAN GOGH MUSEUM

Visiting this vast collection of canvases by Vincent van Gogh (1853–90) is as much a tour through the driven painter's troubled mind as it is a tour through his body of work. More than 200 paintings are arranged chronologically, starting with his early career in dreary old Holland – and sombre, depressive paintings like *The Potato Eaters* – and ending less than a decade later in sunny Arles, where he produced his best-known work with his characteristic giddy, intense colour. Van Gogh committed suicide in 1890 at the age of 37 (not long after famously cutting off his own ear during a dispute with Paul Gauguin), and he sold only one painting in his lifetime.

The museum opened in 1973 to house Theo van Gogh's collection of his brother's paintings, drawings and sketchbooks, and some 800 letters written by the artist. These are complemented by a small selection of paintings by contemporaries, most of whom were friends, such as Toulouse-Lautrec and Gauguin, or artists he admired, such as Jean-François Millet. This is all laid out in a blocky building by premier Dutch architect Gerrit Rietveld, and the museum also hosts superb temporary exhibitions in a separate Kisho Kurokawa–designed wing (dubbed 'The Mussel' by locals). See p98 for more information.

>AMSTERDAM DIARY

Understandably for such a rain-sodden city, the busiest time for festivals in Amsterdam is July and August, when performers have the best chance of clear skies. In autumn (September to November), the regular cultural season starts up at the established venues and runs through to spring (March to May). January and February are slow in terms of formal events, but there are only-in-winter perks like ice skating at Museumplein (p96) and hot-chocolate stands around town. For a schedule of events during your visit, pick up the monthly agenda from the Uitburo (p93) or an issue of *Time Out Amsterdam*, also monthly.

Spectators gather for the Grachtenfestival (p24)

JANUARY

Amsterdam International Fashion Week

www.aifw.nl

Amsterdam's fledgling fashion scene takes flight with events around the city, but is based primarily at Westergasfabriek. Unlike many fashion weeks, there's a substantial program open to the public.

FEBRUARY

Februaristaking

A commemoration of the dock workers' strike of 25 February 1941, to protest the German occupation and the persecution of Jews. There's a ceremony at the *Dokwerker* statue next to the Portuguese-Israelite Synagogue (p124).

MARCH

5 Days Off

www.5daysoff.nl

Electronic music gets its due at this fest in the major club venues. The programming is edgier and more selective than Amsterdam Dance Event (p25), and the feeling more intimate.

Stille Omgang

www.stille-omgang.nl

Thousands attend this silent march commemorating the 1345 Miracle of Amsterdam (p41).

APRIL

Amsterdam Fantastic Film Festival

www.afff.nl

Horror, sci-fi, anime and more crowd the screen at this 11-day genre-fest. Screenings take place at the Kriterion cinema in Plantage.

Paint the town orange on Koninginnedag (Queen's Day)

World Press Photo

www.worldpressphoto.org

This gripping display of the year's best photojournalism debuts in the Oude Kerk in late April, and stays on display until June.

Koninginnedag

Queen's Day, 30 April, is a celebration of the House of Orange, with more than 400,000 orange-clad people filling Amsterdam's streets for drinking and dancing. The city also becomes one big flea market, as people sell off all their unwanted junk.

MAY

Art Amsterdam

www.artamsterdam.nl

Formerly known as KunstRAI, this international art fair draws buyers with deep pockets – it's chic and commercial.

Kunstvlaai

www.kunstvlaai.nl

What used to be a fringe version of Art Amsterdam is now a stand-alone event, with some overlapping dates. Expect odd installations, open studios and more.

JUNE

Holland Festival

www.hollandfestival.nl

The winter culture season winds up with a bang at this big-name theatre, dance and opera festival – it acts as the bookend to Uitmarkt (p24).

Amsterdam Roots Festival

www.amsterdamroots.nl

Fantastic world music programming at several big venues for five days, plus free concerts in Oosterpark (p113), in one of the city's most diverse neighbourhoods.

Open Tuinen Dagen

www.opentuinendagen.nl

Grand homes on the canal belt open their gardens to visitors for one weekend near the end of the month.

JULY

Over Het IJ

www.overhetij.nl

The raw industrial space of the NDSM shipyards is the setting for this equally raw theatre festival. Take the ferry over and prepare to be delighted – many of the shows are physical, or in English.

Amsterdam International Fashion Week

www.aifw.nl

The summer edition of the city's fashion festivities (opposite).

Julidans

www.julidans.nl

For the entire month, Amsterdam's substantial modern dance scene is on show – along with international guests – at the city's biggest venues.

Kwakoe
www.kwakoe.nl, in Dutch
Every weekend from early July to mid-August, this massive food-and-football fair celebrates Surinamese culture. It's well worth the trip to the Bijlmer for the spicy treats and music.

AUGUST

Amsterdam Pride
www.amsterdampride.nl
The last weekend in July or the first in August is dedicated to this completely over-the-top gay fest, with a parade on the canals followed by street parties.

De Parade
www.deparade.nl, in Dutch
This cool short-performance theatre fest takes place in a collection of circus tents in Martin Luther King Park. It runs nightly for the first half of the month, and usually includes a lot of physical, non-language-dependent shows.

Grachtenfestival
www.grachtenfestival.nl
Classical music takes to the water in this eight-day festival. The highlight is the free concert on a barge opposite the Pulitzer hotel, attended by nearly every boat in the city.

Y-M-C-A: Take to the canals during Pride

Hartjesdag
A cross-dressing festival with medieval roots, Hartjesdag (Hearts Day) is like a block party for the Zeedijk, on the third weekend of August. Highly festive, and not just a gay scene.

Uitmarkt
www.uitmarkt.nl, in Dutch
At this mega arts event at the end of August, Amsterdam's cultural venues preview their upcoming season on outdoor stages. It's complemented by a couple of big concerts.

SEPTEMBER

Amsterdam Fringe Festival
www.amsterdamfringefestival.nl
Running parallel events with the Theater-festival (right), the increasingly popular

Amsterdam Fringe takes over odd corners of the city, whether smaller theatres or apartment balconies. As many of the performers come from other countries, English is the de facto language for shows.

Jordaan Festival

www.jordaanfestival.nl, in Dutch
Practitioners of the nostalgic, tears-in-your-beer music called *levenslied* – a speciality of the tight-knit Jordaan – take the stage in this late-September weekend event.

Theaterfestival van Nederland en Vlaanderen

www.tf.nl
During the first two weeks of the month, this drama fest takes over most venues in

the city, with a number of productions either in English or accompanied by projected translation.

OCTOBER

Amsterdam Affordable Art Fair

www.affordableartfair.nl
All work must be priced less than €5000 at this showcase for young talent, presented by galleries from around the Netherlands and beyond. It takes place at the Westergasfabriek on the last weekend of the month.

Amsterdam Dance Event

www.amsterdam-dance-event.nl
A club music powwow, with 700 DJs and more than 40,000 avid dancers attending parties all over the city – all on one sweaty weekend late in the month.

ING Amsterdam Marathon

www.ingamsterdammarathon.nl
Some 25,000 runners race around the Rijksmuseum, Vondelpark and other city landmarks – an inspiring route for runners and an inspiring effort for spectators.

NOVEMBER

Cannabis Cup

www.cannabiscup.com
For five days in late November, Amsterdam gives in fully to its reputation as the weed capital of the world. The daytime Cup activities

AT THE MOVIES

In July, and even more so in August, Amsterdam goes crazy for outdoor films. The major options:

> **Pluk de Nacht** (www.plukdenacht .nl) Two-week festival of international film, with screenings on the IJ.

> **Eye** (p103) Classics outdoors in Vondelpark during July and August.

> **Filmhuis Cavia** (www.filmhuis cavia.nl, in Dutch) Seventies classics and other must-sees at a different public space each Saturday in August.

> **Rialto** (www.rialtofilm.nl, in Dutch) At the Marie Heinekenplein in De Pijp for one weekend in late August.

are a hilarious mix of garden show and trade fair; evenings are one long afterparty.

Museumnacht

www.n8.nl

On the first Saturday in November, exhibition halls all over the city keep their doors open till 2am and schedule special performances, activities and parties. It's a good idea to buy tickets ahead – see the website for details.

International Documentary Film Festival

www.idfa.nl

Ten days in late November are dedicated to screening fascinating true stories from all over the world.

Sinterklaas Intocht

www.sintinamsterdam.nl, in Dutch

Marking the beginning of the holiday season in mid-November, Sinterklaas arrives by boat in the harbour and parades through town on his horse, tossing candy and ginger cookies to the city's entire child population. The date shifts each year, with festivities held all weekend.

DECEMBER

Oudejaarsavond

Fireworks-safety posters plaster the city in the month leading up to New Year's Eve, but they're no deterrent: at midnight, Amsterdam explodes with pyrotechnics – try to secure a spot indoors with a view.

Locals enjoy a kick on Museumplein (p96)

ITINERARIES

Amsterdam is compact, so there's no need to focus on one neighbourhood a day – you can hopscotch all over with ease. As walking across the central canal ring takes less than an hour, you can squeeze a lot in, but to get the most out of your time, rent a bicycle (p175).

ONE DAY

Do your duty to art first: spin through the Rijksmuseum (p98) or Van Gogh Museum (p98) before the crowds arrive, then lunch by snacking your way along the Albert Cuypmarkt (p106) or having a late Turkish breakfast at Bazar (p109). Get yourself oriented by strolling the canal ring and browsing the Negen Straatjes (p14). At twilight, venture through De Wallen (the red-light district; p12), and have a drink at In de Olofspoort (p54) or 't Mandje (p56). Then do elegant Dutch at Greetje (p128) or Hemelse Modder (p128).

FORWARD PLANNING

Six months before you go Book your hotel, especially if you'll be visiting in the summer – top choices fill up very fast. (See p148 for some suggestions.)

Two to three months before you go Check the calendars for the Concertgebouw (p102), Muziekgebouw aan 't IJ (p139), Melkweg (p94) and Paradiso (p94) and buy tickets for anything that looks appealing.

Two weeks before you go Make reservations for De Kas (p117) or Bordewijk (p68). Book a massage at Deco Sauna (p77). Check programs of festivals (p22) and arrange a home dinner through www.like-a-local.com. Check recent notes or post your own query at www.facebook.com/greatlittleplaceamsterdam. Take a brush-up spin on a bicycle, and attune your ears to the sound of a bike bell.

A few days before you go Make reservations at your top dinner choice for your first night in town (and your second, if you're organised enough). Buy tickets to the Rijksmuseum (p98), Van Gogh Museum (p98) and Anne Frank Huis (p62) online. Print out cycling tours of the Eastern Docklands (p132) from www.easterndocklands.com, download an audio tram tour (p138) or arrange a walk with Mee in Mokum (p177).

Top left See or be seen in Vondelpark (p18) **Top right** Here's looking at you: an example of Amsterdam's wacky street art
Bottom De Kaaskamer cheese shop (p69) is heaven for cheese-lovers

't Smalle (p77) lies in the heart of the Jordaan and is unrivalled for *gezelligheid*

THREE DAYS

Follow the one-day itinerary, making time to sign up for a tour with the St Nicolaas Boat Club (p178) for your second day. On your second morning, visit Anne Frank Huis (p62), lunch at Spanjer en van Twist (p72), then hop on your boat tour. Call in at the Uitburo (p93) for concert or show tickets, or hit the bars and clubs around the Leidseplein; De Zotte (p74) is a good place for a beer and simple meal beforehand. On day three, start the morning at Gartine (p48), then pop back over to De Wallen to see the Oude Kerk (p43). Lunch at grand cafe De Jaren (p47), and check out the scene at Vondelpark (p99). Have a casual dinner in the Jordaan at Festina Lente (p69), then enjoy a beer or two at 't Smalle (p77) or De Kat in de Wijngaert (p73).

WET WEATHER

Imagine yourself in sunnier climes at the Tropenmuseum (p113), then – if it's winter – go ice skating at Museumplein (p96). Visit Deco Sauna (p77) to warm up again, and keep the glow going with a hearty Dutch meal at Moeders (p70) or rib-sticking fondue at Café Bern (p127). Get your fix of *gezelligheid,* the cosy Dutch atmosphere that flourishes under grey skies, at any number of 'brown cafes' (p160). A *kopstot* (a shot of Dutch-style gin with a side of beer) works wonders. Then dance the night away at Paradiso (p94) or Melkweg (p94).

OFFBEAT AMSTERDAM
Visit specialised collections like the Bijbels Museum (p62) or the Tassenmuseum Hendrikje (p85), and see Ons' Lieve Heer op Solder (p43), a church hidden in an attic. Continue the theme with Dutch-style pancakes at tiny Pannenkoekenhuis Upstairs (p51). Chill out with a joint and peruse the thrift goods at Sanementereng (p75), or head to De Looier (p65) for even more junk-cum-antiques. Submit to the chef's whims at a set-menu restaurant such as Gare de l'Est (p137) or Balthazar's Keuken (p68), or eat at squat restaurant De Peper (p101). Finally, check out whatever's on in the performance space at OT301 (p103).

FUN FOR FREE
Pop into the Begijnhof (p40), a hidden courtyard, and stroll through the Amsterdams Historisch Museum's Civic Guard Gallery (p40) to get your Golden Age fix (also admire the David and Goliath figures in the museum cafe). Attend a midday concert at the Concertgebouw (p102), learn all about the city's contemporary architecture at the Zuiderkerk (p125) and ARCAM (p133), then take in the view from the top of the Openbare Bibliotheek Amsterdam (public library; p136). People-watch at Vondelpark (p99), and join the Friday Night Skate (p99) from here, for an in-line tour through the city.

>NEIGHBOURHOODS

If you find a free table at De Jaren (p47), grab it quick!

NEIGHBOURHOODS

Amsterdam is a city that rewards aimless wandering. Narrow alleys contain random art installations. Views shift as you mount canal bridges. And the Dutch custom of curtainless windows seems designed to entertain flâneurs (and voyeurs).

That's good, because you'll almost certainly get lost. There's never a straight line in this town, just a zigzag of short streets and curving canals. The Centrum (the city centre) contains De Wallen (the red-light district), a bizarre juxtaposition of the modern sex industry with picturesque centuries-old buildings. In the Centrum's newer half, the city's intellectual life converges around the Spui, a square flanked by cafes and bookshops.

The Western Canal Belt is where dedicated shoppers spend their days, hopping from odd boutique to waterside cafe. To the west of here, the Jordaan is Amsterdam's Greenwich Village, a gentrified bohemia that is one of the best places in the city to get lost.

The canal ring completes its half-loop south of the centre. By day, visit the Southern Canal Belt's obscure museums; by night, party at the clubs around the area's two main squares. Just beyond the canals, Vondelpark is a green lung with personality, adjacent to the Old South, a genteel, quiet area that is a fitting home for the city's grandest museums. Next door, ethnic meets trendy in De Pijp, a neighbourhood where eateries serve cuisine from the Netherlands' former colonies.

Amsterdam's east side begins at the Nieuwmarkt and extends into the leafy expanse of the Plantage, the greenest area in this verdant city. Come here to browse the Waterlooplein flea market or to see the traces of Amsterdam's Jewish heritage. The highlight of the multiethnic Oosterpark district, just beyond, is the excellent Tropenmuseum.

In Amsterdam's harbour, the ever-changing skyline includes a state-of-the-art concert hall and extends into the edgy Eastern Docklands, adored by the design clique for its architectural experimentation.

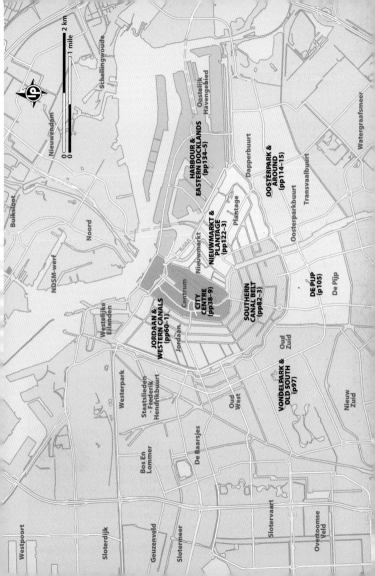

>CITY CENTRE

The medieval core of Amsterdam is split down the middle by the Damrak. To the east lies the Oude Zijde (Old Side), with De Wallen (the red-light district) at its northern end. Far from being a no-go area, it has some beautiful historical bars, as well as the stunning Oude Kerk (p43), the city's oldest church. The Zeedijk, on the northeast side, marks the location of the city's old sea wall. Since the late 19th century, it has been Amsterdam's Chinatown, but it's also a symbol of urban rebirth: in the 1980s, the street was a major junkie hangout, but it's now home to a Buddhist temple, tiny boutiques and some excellent bars. South of the Dam, the skinny Nes was once a long row of monasteries; now it's the theatre district. At the southern end of the Oude Zijde, the University of Amsterdam (UvA) occupies a cluster of grand old buildings.

West of the Damrak, the Nieuwe Zijde (New Side) is only a century or so younger, but it does feel noticeably more modern. Trams run along filled-in canals, and the city's main mass-market shopping streets, Nieuwendijk and Kalverstraat, are a swath of chain shops. But in the tiny alleys connecting the main avenues, which are barely wide enough for two people to pass, you'll find surprising bars and cafes. The Spui, a plaza near the south end of the area, is an intellectual hub for the city – there's more UvA campus over here, several excellent bookshops and a weekly book market. The numerous casual cafe-bars in the area cater both to students and after-work beer-drinkers.

The Damrak, one of the city centre's busiest thoroughfares

CITY CENTRE

🟢 SEE

Amsterdams
  Historisch Museum **1** B7
Begijnhof **2** B7
Beurs van Berlage **3** D4
Civic Guard Gallery **4** B7
Dam Square & Nationaal
  Monument **5** C5
Guan Yin Shrine **6** E5
Koninklijk Paleis **7** B5
Madame Tussauds **8** B5
Nieuwe Kerk **9** B5
Noord/Zuidlijn
  Viewpoint **10** B7
Ons' Lieve Heer
  op Solder **11** D4
Oude Kerk **12** D5
Prostitution
  Information Centre **13** D4
Schreierstoren **14** E3

🏠 SHOP

Athenaeum **15** A7
Condomerie **16** C5
Conscious Dreams
  Kokopelli **17** D4
De Bijenkorf **18** C5
Female & Partners **19** B4
Fred de la Bretonière ...**20** B6
Geels & Co **21** D4
Hans Appenzeller **22** C7
HEMA **23** B8
HEMA **24** C4

Jacob Hooy & Co **25** E6
Laundry Industry **26** B7
Laundry Industry **27** B5
Maison de
  Bonneterie **28** B8
Mark Raven Grafiek **29** B5
Open **30** B6
Oudemanhuispoort
  Book Market **31** C7
Outland Records **32** E4
PGC Hajenius **33** B7
Sissy-Boy **34** B5
Wonderwood **35** D7

🍴 EAT

De Bakkerswinkel **36** D4
De Jaren **37** C8
De Keuken van 1870 ....**38** C3
Dop **39** B7
Gartine **40** B7
Gebr Niemeijer **41** C3
Hofje van Wijs **42** E4
Kam Yin **43** E4
Kapitein Zeppo's **44** C7
La Place **45** C8
Lanskroon **46** A7
Lucius **47** A7
Nam Kee **48** E5
Nyonya **49** D6
Pannenkoekenhuis
  Upstairs **50** C7
Rob Wigboldus
  Vishandel **51** C5
'Skek **52** E4

Supperclub **53** B6
Thais Snackbar Bird **54** E4
Van Kerkwijk **55** C6
Villa Zeezicht **56** B5
Vlaams Frites Huis **57** B8

🍷 DRINK

Abraxas **58** B6
Bar Italia **59** C6
Crea **60** C7
Dampkring **61** B8
De Prael **62** D4
Getto **63** D4
Gollem **64** A7
Greenhouse **65** C6
Hoppe **66** A7
In 't Aepjen **67** E3
In de Olofspoort **68** E3
In de Wildeman **69** C4
Kadinsky **70** B7
Latei **71** E5
Schuim **72** A6
't Mandje **73** E4
Vrankrijk **74** A6
Wynand Fockink **75** C6

⭐ PLAY

Bitterzoet **76** C3
Casa Rosso **77** D5
Casablanca **78** E4
Winston Kingdom **79** D5

Please see over for map

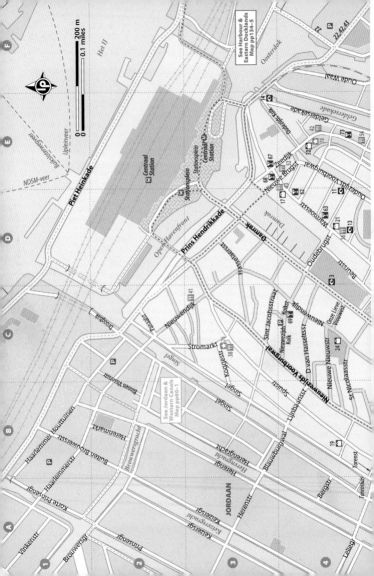

◉ SEE

◉ AMSTERDAMS HISTORISCH MUSEUM

☎ 523 18 22; www.ahm.nl; Nieuwezijds Voorburgwal 357; admission €10/5; ◷ 10am-5pm Mon-Fri, 11am-5pm Sat & Sun; 🚊 1/2/5 Spui; ♿

You won't find any dusty relics here – the city's history museum covers the early years well, but just as interesting are the exhibits on the past century. You can peek into typical Amsterdam apartments, hear immigrants' stories and even visit a recreation of 't Mandje (p56), the historic gay bar. Don't miss the **Civic Guard Gallery** (free entrance) in the alley on the southern side of the museum, which is lined with grand posed group portraits from the Dutch Golden Age.

◉ BEGIJNHOF

☎ 622 19 18; www.begijnhofamster dam.nl; Spui; ◷ 8am-5pm; 🚊 1/2/5 Spui; ♿

This quiet courtyard and the houses around it were built for the Beguines, a lay Catholic sisterhood. After the Protestant Alteration in 1578, the women worshipped in a chapel hidden in a house. It is decorated with paintings depicting the Miracle of Amsterdam (boxed text, opposite). English Puritans took over the church in the yard; look for pulpit panels by Piet Mondrian, in a figurative phase. The last of the sisters died in 1971, but the houses here are still reserved for women. In the hallway from the Spui, look for carvings of dogs, chickens and men – all things prohibited here, in order to keep the peace.

Mingle with the pigeons on the Dam

MMM, TASTY – & MIRACULOUS!

In 1345 a dying man received the final sacrament, but he later vomited up the Host (communion wafer). His nurse tossed the mess in the fire, but the Host would not burn – and the man was shortly restored to health. Once word got out about the miraculous flame-retardant wafer and its healing powers, pilgrims flocked to Amsterdam; even future Hapsburg emperor Maximilian came to be healed in the 15th century. Paintings and a mural depicting the Miracle of Amsterdam hang in the chapel in the Begijnhof (opposite), and every year on 12 March, the Stille Omgang (Silent Procession) along the Heiligeweg honours the event, with thousands of people attending.

◐ BEURS VAN BERLAGE
☎ 530 41 41; www.bvb.nl; Damrak 277;
🕙 10am-6pm Mon-Sat, 11am-6pm Sun;
🚊 4/9/16/24/25 Dam

Master architect and ardent socialist HP Berlage (1856–1934) built this financial exchange in 1903. He filled the temple of capitalism with decorations that venerate labour – look inside the cafe to see tile murals of the well-muscled proletariat of the past, present and future. The present bourse is located across the street, and this building now contains concert halls and expo space; tours are available by appointment through Artifex (p178).

◐ DAM SQUARE & NATIONAAL MONUMENT
Dam; 🚊 4/9/16/24/25 Dam

This pigeon-filled expanse was the site of the original dam built across the Amstel. Now it is busker central, with the occasional puppet show during summer months and a Ferris wheel in the spring. The obelisk on the east side is the Nationaal Monument, which was built in 1956 to honour the fallen of WWII.

◐ GUAN YIN SHRINE
Fo Guang Shan He Hua Temple; ☎ 420 23 57; www.ibps.nl; Zeedijk 106-118;
🕙 noon-5pm Tue-Sat, 10am-5pm Sun;
🚊 4/9/16/24/25 Dam

Opened in 2000, this Buddhist temple was the first in the Netherlands. The ornate 'mountain gate' brings a bit of high-altitude Asia to these lowlands, though the interior is relatively small and spare. Sutras (sayings of the Buddha) are recited every Sunday at 10.30am, and there are tours on Saturday at 2pm, 3pm and 4pm.

◎ KONINKLIJK PALEIS

**Royal Palace; ☎ 620 40 60; www
.paleisamsterdam.nl; Dam; admission
€7.50/6.50; ⏱ noon-5pm Tue-Sun;
🚋 4/9/16/24/25 Dam;** ♿

Commissioned as a town hall
in 1648, this building became a
palace in the 19th century. After
recent renovation, the interiors
gleam – especially the marble
work, at its best in a floor inlaid
with maps of the world. Queen
Beatrix uses the palace only for
ceremonies; check the website for
periodic closures.

◎ MADAME TUSSAUDS

**☎ 522 10 10; www.madametussauds.nl;
Dam 20; admission €21/16; ⏱ 10am-
5.30pm; 🚋 4/9/16/24/25 Dam**

Tourism juggernaut Madame
Tussauds is overpriced, but its
focus on local culture makes it fun:
'meet' Dutch royals, politicians,
painters and pop stars, along with
global celebs. Buy tickets online
and go after 3pm for discounts.

◎ NIEUWE KERK

**☎ 638 69 09; www.nieuwekerk.nl;
Dam; admission €12; ⏱ 10am-6pm;
🚋 1/2/5/13/14/17 Raadhuisstraat;** ♿

When not hosting coronations
and royal weddings, the New
Church (dating from 1408 – it's all
relative) exhibits treasures from
other countries, along with an
amazing 10m-tall wood pulpit.
Slip through the gift shop and
upstairs for a free exhibit on the
church's history.

◎ NOORD/ZUIDLIJN VIEWPOINT

**admission free; ⏱ 1-6pm Tue-Sat;
🚋 4/9/14/16/24/25 Rokin**

Any fan of massive engineering
projects should descend the stairs
across from Rokin 96 to see the
north–south metro line excava-

OLD AMSTERDAM MEETS NEW

In the spring of 1609, explorer Henry Hudson sailed his ship *De
Halve Maan* (The Half Moon) from Amsterdam's harbour and off to
the New World, where he found the ideal spot for a trading post.
This became New Amsterdam, capital of New Netherland. Four
hundred years (and a treaty with the British) later, it's better known
as New York, but historians argue that the early Amsterdam expats
are responsible for making the city what it is today: a multiethnic,
business-first metropolis. Just like Amsterdam, but bigger – and
without so many bicycles. You can read all about it in Russell Shorto's excellent history *The Island at the Centre of the World*.

tion in action. Guides can explain the complexities. Look for the big red 'M' next to the bike path. Fascinated? There's even more info (partially in English) at an **office** (🕒 10am-5pm Tue-Fri, 11am-4pm Sun) on the east end of Centraal Station.

🅲 ONS' LIEVE HEER OP SOLDER

Museum Amstelkring; ☎ 624 66 04; www.museumamstelkring.nl; Oudezijds Voorburgwal 40; admission €7/1; 🕒 10am-5pm Mon-Sat, 1-5pm Sun; 🚊 4/9/16/24/25 Centraal Station

Built in 1661 during the Calvinist era, Our Lord in the Attic was a Catholic church hidden on the upper floors of a canal house. A tour of the whole house, via labyrinthine staircases, passes through simple living spaces, a snug 'between room' and into the soaring, two-storey church, complete with organ. From outside, it's difficult to see how everything fits into the skinny building.

🅲 OUDE KERK

☎ 625 82 84; www.oudekerk.nl; Oudekerksplein 23; admission €5/4; 🕒 11am-5pm Mon-Sat, 1-5pm Sun; 🚊 4/9/16/24/25 Dam; ♿

The city's oldest building and earliest parish church was established in 1200, though it was rebuilt in stone a century later. In the ceiling, some of the dark wood boards

date from 1480, and images of saints still glow faintly. Sunday services are held at 11am, but the church generally hosts exhibitions such as the World Press Photo exhibit every April. Outside, look in the cobblestones for a bronze panel of a breast, a bit of anonymous guerrilla art. You can also climb the **tower** (admission €6; 🕒 1-5pm Thu-Sat Apr-Sep).

🅲 PROSTITUTION INFORMATION CENTRE

☎ 420 73 28; www.pic-amsterdam.com; Enge Kerksteeg 3; 🕒 noon-7pm Tue-Sat; 🚊 4/9/16/24/25 Dam

Burning questions about the red-light district? Head to this nonprofit organisation for frank answers, provided by current and former sex workers. There's a small exhibit on prostitution in addition to books on the subject and a few gifts. Better, though, is the excellent **walking tour** (€12.50; 🕒 5pm Sat), which takes you into a working window brothel.

🅲 SCHREIERSTOREN

☎ 428 82 91; Prins Hendrikkade 94-95; 🚊 4/9/16/24/25 Centraal Station

Built around 1480 as part of the city's defences, this brick tower became a point from which women waved farewell to ships. Inside, in the nautical-theme VOC Café, look for a 1569 stone plaque depicting such a woman – she's probably weeping because, in those days, only one in three sailors ever returned safely from a sea journey. Outside, a plaque commemorates Henry Hudson's sailing from here (see the boxed text, p42).

🏠 SHOP

🏠 ATHENAEUM *Books*
☎ 514 14 60; Spui 14-16; 🚋 1/2/5 Spui
Amsterdam's savviest bookshop is a bit of an intellectual and style hub. Its adjoining newsagency has cutting-edge international magazines, newspapers and guidebooks.

🏠 CONDOMERIE *Sex Shop*
☎ 627 41 74; Warmoesstraat 141;
🕐 Mon-Sat; 🚋 4/9/16/24/25 Dam
Putting the 'pro' back in prophylactic: rarely can you shop for a condom in such a tasteful setting, with such a fabulous (borderline mind-boggling) selection. Grab a mixed trial pack if you can't decide.

🏠 CONSCIOUS DREAMS KOKOPELLI *Smart Shop*
☎ 421 70 00; Warmoesstraat 12;
🕐 11am-8pm; 🚋 4/9/16/24/25 Centraal Station
The city's oldest and most reputable smart shop, stocked with 'truffles' (a magic-mushroom alternative) and other herbal inspirations.

🏠 DE BIJENKORF *Department Store*
☎ 621 80 80; Dam 1; 🕐 11am-7pm Mon, 10am-7pm Tue & Wed, 10am-9pm Thu & Fri, 9.30am-7pm Sat, noon-7pm Sun; 🚋 4/9/16/24/25 Dam
The prestigious 'Beehive', established in 1850, is indeed a busy place, its five floors packed with designer brands from home (G-Star Raw Denim, for instance) and

QUICK(IE) FACTS
In De Wallen (the red-light district), prostitution is an industry like any other. You'll see specialisation – an NL sticker in a window, indicating 'Dutch spoken here', and sections occupied by women from Suriname, Russia or Latin America – and of course aggressive self-marketing. Women pay between €75 and €150 to rent a window for an eight- or 10-hour shift (the rate depends on the facilities, but all rooms have a bed and a sink), and charge between €35 and €50 for a blowjob or a quickie (15 minutes or less). They also pay income taxes based on city estimates of income correlated with tourism figures. No wonder – allegedly some 40% of the customers are British.

In Amsterdam, fun comes in all shapes and sizes

abroad (DKNY etc). The top-floor cafeteria offers good fresh food, and there's an outdoor area.

FEMALE & PARTNERS
Sex Shop

🕐 1-6.30pm Mon, 11am-6.30pm Tue, Wed & Fri, 11am-9pm Thu, 11am-6pm Sat, 1-6pm Sun

The sign on the door says 'Push (harder)', setting the tone for this sex-toy shop that doesn't take itself too seriously. It stocks nontrashy lingerie and body jewellery designed by the female owners, along with vibrators, toys and DVDs.

FRED DE LA BRETONIÈRE
Footwear

☎ 623 41 52; Sint Luciënsteeg 20;
🚊 1/2/5/14 Paleisstraat

This Dutch shoe designer's products are solid, as if made to ride a bicycle in. That sounds dull, but in fact Fred satisfies the burning need for a sensible heel and a knee-high boot in candy-apple red leather. Men's shoes are also available, though the colour spectrum isn't as broad.

GEELS & CO *Food & Drink*

☎ 624 06 83; Warmoesstraat 67;
🕐 9.30am-6pm Mon-Sat;
🚊 4/9/16/24/25 Dam

The distinguished Geels & Co has been roasting coffees and selling loose-leaf tea for 140 years. Not only does it smell great, but there are charming teapots, coffee pots and brewing paraphernalia for sale.

HANS APPENZELLER
Jewellery

☎ 626 82 18; Grimburgwal 1;
🕐 Tue-Sat; 🚊 4/9/14/16/24/25 Spui

One of Amsterdam's leading designers in gold and stone; if the work is not your style, check out the other jewellers along the street.

HEMA *Clothing, Housewares*

☎ 623 41 76; Nieuwendijk 174;
🕐 10.30am-6.30pm Mon, 9.30am-6.30pm Tue, Wed, Fri & Sat, 9.30am-9pm Thu, noon-6pm Sun; 🚊 4/9/16/24/25 Dam

Check the label on any Dutch behind: HEMA, a Dutch five-and-dime that's as fun as it is functional, is the place to go for underwear…plus kitchen towels, espresso cups and bike accessories. There's another branch at the **Kalvertoren shopping centre** (Kalverstraat 212).

☐ JACOB HOOY & CO
Perfume & Cosmetics
☎ 624 30 41; Kloveniersburgwal 12; ⏰ Mon-Sat; 🚊 4/9/16/24/25 Dam
This chemist's shop has been selling medicinal herbs, homeopathic remedies and natural cosmetics since 1743, and its interior, lined with wooden drawers, has barely changed.

☐ LAUNDRY INDUSTRY
Clothing
☎ 420 25 54; Spui 1; 🚊 4/9/14/16/24/25 Spui
This cool Dutch label specialises in minimalist functional fashion in neutrals, but with attractive details like pintucking and shirring. There's another in **Magna Plaza** (Spuistraat 137).

☐ MAISON DE BONNETERIE
Department Store
☎ 531 34 00; Rokin 140; 🚊 4/9/14/16/24/25 Muntplein
Amsterdam's establishment, including Queen Beatrix, likes to shop at this grand old department store. A bit flashier and more exclusive than De Bijenkorf (p44-5).

☐ MARK RAVEN GRAFIEK
Souvenirs
☎ 330 08 00; Nieuwezijds Voorburgwal 174; 🚊 1/2/5/13/14/17 Dam/Raadhuisstraat
Artist Raven's distinctive vision of Amsterdam is available as posters and on T-shirts – they make genuinely tasteful souvenirs. He also has a stand on Museumplein.

☐ OPEN *Clothing*
☎ 528 69 63; Nieuwezijds Voorburgwal 291; ⏰ noon-7pm Fri-Wed, noon-9pm Thu; 🚊 1/2/5/14 Paleisstraat
This tiny shop showcases 10 different designers – a bit of repurposed vintage chic, a bit of creative knit jersey, and some tongue-in-cheek Dutch milkmaid skirts. We like 100% Halal, a line of East-meets-West street style.

☐ OUDEMANHUIS BOOK MARKET *Books*
Oudemanhuispoort; ⏰ 11am-4pm Mon-Fri; 🚊 4/9/14/16/24/25 Spui
A favourite with academics, this moody old covered alleyway is lined with secondhand booksellers. Most of the material is in Dutch, but one vendor specialises in cookbooks, many in English.

☐ OUTLAND RECORDS *Music*
☎ 638 75 76; Zeedijk 22; ⏰ 11am-7pm Mon-Sat, 11am-9pm Thu, noon-6pm Sun; 🚊 4/9/16/24/25 Centraal Station

A purist's club-music shop with vinyl only, plus designer Japanese toys and rhinestone-encrusted headphones. Get info and tickets for parties here.

🏬 PGC HAJENIUS
Speciality Shop

☎ 623 74 94; Rokin 96;
🚃 4/9/14/16/24/25 Spui

Even if you're not a cigar connoisseur, stroll through this tobacco emporium for a glimpse of the grandeur that used to line the Rokin in the early 20th century. Inside is all art deco stained glass, gilt trim and soaring ceilings. Regular customers, including members of the Dutch royal family, have private humidors here.

🏬 SISSY-BOY
Clothing, Housewares

☎ 389 25 89; Spuistraat 137; 🕑 11am-7pm Mon, 10am-7pm Tue-Sat, to 9pm Thu, noon-7pm Sun; 🚃 1/2/5/13/14/17 Raadhuisstraat

Never mind the name – this Dutch clothing chain sells quirky print shirts and other items that tread the line between preppie and hip. This large branch in the basement of the Magna Plaza shopping centre also stocks lots of home items.

🏬 WONDERWOOD *Design*

☎ 625 37 38; Rusland 3; 🕑 noon-6pm Wed-Sat; 🚃 4/9/14/16/24/25 Spui

As much a museum as a shop, here you can ogle the sensuous, delicate moulded-plywood creations of George Nelson, Marcel Breuer and more – some of the vintage pieces are for sale, and some available in reissue. If that's impractical, smaller art objects (made of wood, naturally) are also available.

🍴 EAT

🍴 DE BAKKERSWINKEL
Cafe & Bakery €

☎ 489 80 00; Warmoesstraat 69;
🕑 8am-6pm Tue-Fri, 8am-5pm Sat, 10am-5pm Sun; 🚃 4/9/16/24/25 Dam;
Ⓥ ♿

Right on the hot-and-heavy Warmoesstraat is this family-friendly cafe with excellent baked goods, especially scones. There's a kids' play area out back.

🍴 DE JAREN *Cafe* €

☎ 625 57 71; Nieuwe Doelenstraat 20-22; 🕑 10am-1am; 🚃 4/9/14/16/24/25 Muntplein; Ⓥ ♿

This big, buzzy and bright bar-cafe-restaurant is one of the city's best, thanks in part to its handy location and two large terraces on the water. It's the kind of place where you head for a coffee and end up leaving hours later having consumed an entire magazine, a satisfying sandwich and a glass or two of wine.

🍴 DE KEUKEN VAN 1870
Dutch   €

☎ 620 40 18; Spuistraat 4; 🕑 lunch &
dinner Mon-Sat; 🚊 1/2/5/13/17 Martelaarsgracht; Ⓥ ♿

Though it's white and airy inside,
rather than wood-panelled, this
bargain restaurant is as Dutch as
it comes. The three-course set
menu (€8.50) involves *stamppot*
(mashed veg and potatoes) and
vla (pudding). Bachelors read
newspapers and sip glasses of
milk. A cat roams around. And the
service is surly – just consider that
a cultural experience.

🍴 DOP *Sandwich Shop*   €

☎ 624 75 51; Taksteeg 6; 🕑 10.30am-
5.30pm Mon, 10am-5.30pm Tue-Fri,
10am-6pm Thu, 11am-7pm Sat;
🚊 4/9/14/16/24/25 Spui

Sandwiches at Dop may look
simple, but they're certainly not
skimpy – your white roll comes
slathered with plenty of butter and an ample portion of, for
example, leg of lamb, roast beef
or liverwurst. With a side of *frites*
(that, dare we say, beat those at
Vlaams Frites Huis, p53), you have
a real workhorse Dutch lunch.

🍴 GARTINE *Cafe*   €

☎ 320 41 32; Taksteeg 7; 🕑 10am-6pm
Wed-Sun; 🚊 4/9/14/16/24/25 Spui; Ⓥ

Gartine makes delectable
breakfast pastries, sandwiches

and salads from produce grown
in its own garden plot. Throw
into the mix the cafe's slow-food
credentials and gorgeous antique
plates and it's a winner, and a rare
bright spot in the dull Kalverstraat area.

🍴 GEBR NIEMEIJER
Cafe   €

☎ 707 67 52; Nieuwendijk 35;
🕑 8.15am-6.30pm Tue-Fri, 8.30am-5pm
Sat, 9.30am-5pm Sun; 🚊 1/2/5/13/17
Martelaarsgracht; ♿ Ⓥ

An oasis of tastefulness amid the
Nieuwendijk's head shops, this
French bakery is a great breakfast
spot. On busy days, the tables can
be littered with shards of flaky
croissants – a small price to pay
for quality pastry. For lunch, try
the fig-walnut bread with gruyère
cheese.

🍴 HOFJE VAN WIJS *Cafe*   €

☎ 624 04 36; Zeedijk 43; 🕑 noon-6pm
Tue, Wed & Sun, noon-10.30pm Thu &
Fri, 10am-10.30pm Sat; 🚊 4/9/16/24/25
Centraal Station

The 200-year-old coffee and tea
vendor Wijs & Zonen maintains
this pretty courtyard cafe. In
addition to housemade cakes, it
serves seasonal Dutch treats, such
as spring asparagus. The place
also runs a weekly **walking tour**
(🕑 2.30pm Sat), which begins with
coffee and *appeltaart*.

Berna Meijer
Tour guide at the Prostitution Information Centre (p43)

Loving her Job No question is taboo. Like, I asked a prostitute, 'What's "the turtle"'? She said, 'Get on the floor…'. **Relax** It's OK to look. But there's a difference between looking and staring – you're not at a zoo. Give a smile – they're normal women, and they appreciate it. **Don't miss…** Look at the crooked buildings, and details like the boobie by the Oude Kerk (p43). **Best time** In the summer, when it's just getting dark – you really taste the bubbly vibe. **Best eats** Kam Yin (p50) is very cheap and has the best roti. **Best bar** Casablanca (p57)! It's great for karaoke, but don't go if you're claustrophobic. **A quieter drink** In de Olofspoort (p54) has old-fashioned liqueurs with weird names, like the 'missy in green'. **Best sex show** Casa Rosso (p57) really tries to make women feel comfortable.

☷ KAM YIN *Surinamese* €
☎ 625 31 15; Warmoesstraat 8; ☷ noon-midnight; ☷ 4/9/16/24/25 Centraal Station; Ⓥ ☷

It's nothing much to look at, but this plastic and fluorescent operation nonetheless dispenses excellent versions of Surinamese standards like roti and *tjauw min* (thick noodles with assorted meats). Its *broodje pom* (a chicken-casserole sandwich) rivals De Tokoman's (p128).

☷ KAPITEIN ZEPPO'S
Cafe €€
☎ 624 20 57; Gebed Zonder End 5; ☷ lunch & dinner; ☷ 4/9/14/16/24/25 Spui; ☷

In an alley off Grimburgwal, this bar-cafe has a timeless bohemian feel, whether at the tiletop, candlelit tables or in the covered winter garden. There's a light brasserie menu, and the restaurant upstairs is also good, featuring Amsterdam's best waiters (a crew of older Italian men).

☷ LA PLACE *Cafe* €
☎ 235 83 63; Kalverstraat 203; ☷ 11am-8pm Sun & Mon, 10am-8pm Mon-Wed, Fri & Sat, 10am-9pm Thu; ☷ 4/9/14/16/24/25 Muntplein; ☷ Ⓥ ☷

On the 1st floor of the Vroom & Dreesmann department store, this deluxe cafeteria has a little something for everyone: sandwiches, quiches, stir-fries, pastas, all freshly prepared. The ground-floor Le Marché has takeaway sandwiches.

☷ LANSKROON
Bakery & Sweets €
☎ 623 77 43; Singel 385; ☷ 8am-5.30pm Mon-Fri, 9am-5.30pm Sat, 10am-5.30pm Sun; ☷ 1/2/5 Spui; Ⓥ ☷

Other historic bakeries have prettier fixtures and daintier cakes, but only humble Lanskroon has such a remarkable *stroopwafel* – crispy, big as a dessert plate and available with caramel, honey or a deceptively healthy-tasting fig paste. In winter, locals come for spicy *speculaas* biscuits and other holiday treats, and there's ice cream in the summer.

☷ LUCIUS *Seafood* €€
☎ 624 18 31; Spuistraat 247; ☷ 5pm-midnight; ☷ 1/2/5 Spui

Delicious and consistently full, Lucius is known for simple but expertly prepared fish, such as Dover sole in butter and giant North Sea oysters. The interior, decked-out with fish tanks and tiles, is workmanlike and professional, just like the service. It's perhaps a little more expensive than it ought to be, but it's also a rare restaurant that's open so late.

☷ NAM KEE *Chinese* €
☎ 624 34 70; Zeedijk 111-113; ☷ noon-11pm; ☷ 4/9/16/24/25 Dam; Ⓥ

Nam Kee's steamed oysters with black-bean sauce are legendary in Amsterdam. They are delicious, but the atmosphere can be grim (and we have a high tolerance for fluorescent lights). A second location nearby (p129) is nicer.

🍴 NYONYA *Malaysian* €
☎ 422 24 47; Kloveniersburgwal 38; ⏲ 1-9pm Wed-Mon; Ⓜ Nieuwmarkt; ♿ Ⓥ

Craving Chinese or Indian? Head for Nyonya to get your fix of both: *laksa* (spicy noodle soup) is piled high with goodies, and the *rendang* curry is complex. No alcohol, but you can sip milky tea or Sarsae, a Chinese root beer.

🍴 PANNENKOEKENHUIS UPSTAIRS *Dutch* €
☎ 626 56 03; Grimburgwal 2; ⏲ noon-5pm; 🚊 4/9/14/16/24/25 Spui; Ⓥ ♿

If you can make it up the steep stairs – then actually find a seat in this tiny place – you'll be able to savour some of the tastiest and least expensive pancakes in town. It's a one-man show, so service operates at its own pace. One other hurdle: it might not always be open during posted hours.

🍴 ROB WIGBOLDUS VISHANDEL *Sandwich Shop* €
☎ 626 33 88; Zoutsteeg 6; ⏲ breakfast & lunch; 🚊 4/9/16/24/25 Dam

A wee oasis in the midst of surrounding tourist tat, this fish shop in a tiny alley serves excellent herring sandwiches (on a choice of crusty white or brown rolls, no less). Don't like fish? Van den Berg, right next door, does all the meaty sandwiches.

🍴 'SKEK *Cafe* €
☎ 427 05 51; Zeedijk 4-8; ⏲ noon-1am Sun-Thu, noon-3am Fri & Sat; 🚊 4/9/16/24/25 Centraal Station; ♿ Ⓥ ♿

Run by students for students (flashing your ID gets you one-third off), this friendly, fun cafe-bar is a nice place to get some healthy food. Bands occasionally perform at night.

🍴 SUPPERCLUB *International* €€€
☎ 344 64 00; www.supperclub.com; Jonge Roelensteeg 21; ⏲ 8pm-1am Sun-Thu, 8pm-3am Fri & Sat; 🚊 1/2/5/14 Paleisstraat; Ⓥ

Supperclub is an Amsterdam institution, but it changes every night. The only certainties are that you'll be served five courses of very high-concept food and people will be performing something around or with you. And you'll have to take your shoes off, as you'll be sprawled on a cushion while it happens. In good weather, take the Supperclub Cruise, on a boat out on the IJ.

NEIGHBOURHOODS

CITY CENTRE

Get down to Getto (p54), a stalwart of the red-light district's gay and lesbian scene

🍴 THAIS SNACKBAR BIRD

Thai €

☎ 420 62 89; Zeedijk 77; 🕑 2-10pm;
🚊 4/9/16/24/25 Centraal Station

Don't tell the Chinese neighbours, but this is some of the best Asian food on the Zeedijk – the cooks, wedged in a tiny kitchen, don't skimp on lemongrass, fish sauce or chilli. There's a bit more room to spread out in the (slightly pricier) restaurant across the street (No 72).

🍴 VAN KERKWIJK

International €€

☎ 620 33 16; Nes 41; 🕑 lunch & dinner;
🚊 4/9/16/24/25 Dam; V 🚹
Exceptionally warm service – your waitress may sit down and chat

before reciting the menu – and interesting, reasonably priced food make this a personal-feeling spot in a somewhat generic part of the city. Although the creative combos don't always hit the mark, the ingredients are fresh and deftly prepared. We recommend the calamari, and the pear tart. Bonus: reservations aren't necessary.

🍴 VILLA ZEEZICHT *Cafe* €

☎ 626 74 33; Torensteeg 7; 🕑 7.30am-9pm; 🚊 1/2/5/13/14/17 Raadhuisstraat;
V 🚹
While Villa Zeezicht does some decent lunch items, it's all just clumsy foreplay for the home-made apple tart with cream that is a deserved Amsterdam legend.

VLAAMS FRITES HUIS
Fast Food €

☎ 624 60 75; Voetboogstraat 33;
🕒 11am-6pm Tue-Sat, noon-6pm Sun & Mon; 🚊 1/2/5 Koningsplein;

Long known as the best place for fried potatoes in Amsterdam, this hole-in-the-wall stand doles them out to *frites* devotees. The sauce selection is vast. (Don't fall for the similarly named place on Handboogstraat.)

▼ DRINK
▼ ABRAXAS *Coffeeshop*
☎ 625 57 63; Jonge Roelensteeg 12;
🕒 10am-1am; 🚊 1/2/5/14 Paleisstraat

The Abraxas management seems to know exactly what stoners want: mellow music, comfy sofas, rooms with different energy levels and, of course, thick milkshakes. The considerate staff and friendly, young clientele make this a fantastic place for coffeeshop newbies. The same owners run a much smaller space at Spuistraat 51.

▼ BAR ITALIA *Cafe, Lounge*
☎ 620 24 42; Rokin 81-83; 🕒 7am-3am Sun-Thu, 7am-4am Fri & Sat;
🚊 4/9/14/16/25 Rokin; V

Amsterdam's chicest grand cafe also has incredibly gener-ous opening hours. You can refuel here, alongside the city's beautiful people, with a morning espresso or a late-night cocktail. Bonus: the kitchen is open late (till 11pm).

▼ CREA *Cafe*
☎ 525 14 23; Turfdraagsterpad 17;
🕒 10am-1am Mon-Sat, 11am-7pm Sun;
🚊 4/9/14/16/24/25 Spui; V

Walking along Grimburgwal, you can't help but notice the prime cafe chairs positioned across the canal. They're part of the University of Amsterdam's cultural centre, which is a laid-back spot with an excellent view of the bridge once known as *the* place to purchase a stolen bike – you might still witness the occasional transaction.

▼ DAMPKRING *Coffeeshop*
☎ 638 07 05; Handboogstraat 29;
🕒 10am-1am; 🚊 1/2/5 Koningsplein

Most famous for its cameo in *Ocean's Twelve*, the moodily lit Dampkring also has a solid selection of weed and helpful staff. The company has expanded its special *dampkring* (atmosphere) to a nearby shop at Heisteeg 6 (signed as De Tweede Kamer, and sporting an excellent art deco interior), and another where Heisteeg meets Singel.

☿ DE PRAEL *Beer Bar*

☎ 408 44 70; Warmoesstraat 15; ⏲ 11-8pm Wed-Sat; ⛴ 4/9/16/24/25 Centraal Station

Sample organic beers named after classic Dutch singers at this spacious, wood-panelled tasting room decorated with old radios and album covers. Each round comes with a warm snack – a generous touch usually unheard-of in Amsterdam. For tours, head around the corner to the brewery itself, at Oudezijds Voorburgwal 30.

☿ GETTO *Gay & Lesbian*

☎ 421 51 51; Warmoesstraat 51; ⏲ 5pm-1am Tue-Sun; ⛴ 4/9/16/24/25 Centraal Station

Getto is a haven for a younger gay and lesbian crowd and anyone who wants a little bohemian subculture in the middle of De Wallen (the red-light district). Its inclusive feel is aided by the two-for-one daily happy hour from 5pm to 7pm; food is good and cheap too.

☿ GOLLEM *Beer Bar*

☎ 626 66 45; Raamsteeg 4; ⛴ 1/2/5 Spui

All the brew-related paraphernalia in this miniscule space barely leaves room for the 200 beers – mostly from Belgium – and the connoisseurs who come to try them. The bartenders are happy to advise.

☿ GREENHOUSE *Coffeeshop*

☎ 627 17 39; Oudezijds Voorburgwal 191; ⏲ 10am-1am; ⛴ 4/9/16/24/25 Dam

This branch of the original in De Pijp (p111) is decorated just as nicely, making it the classiest place in De Wallen. This one has no fiddly 'membership' business.

☿ HOPPE *Brown Cafe*

☎ 420 44 20; Spui 18; ⏲ 8am-1am Mon-Thu, 8am-2am Fri & Sat; ⛴ 1/2/5 Spui

Boasting the city's highest beer turnover, this busy spot has been in business since 1670. Its cosy interior tends to attract as many camera-wielding tourists as locals, but you can dodge the crowds out front through a side entrance on Heisteeg, which leads into the snug tasting room for *jenever* (Dutch-style gin).

☿ IN DE OLOFSPOORT

Tasting House

☎ 624 39 18; Nieuwebrugsteeg 13; ⏲ 4-10pm Thu-Sat; ⛴ 4/9/16/24/25 Centraal Station

Head here for more heady liqueurs after Wynand Fockink (p56) shuts. A crew of regulars has dedicated bottles stocked just for them.

☿ IN DE WILDEMAN *Beer Bar*

☎ 638 23 48; Kolksteeg 3; ⏲ noon-1am Mon-Thu, noon-2am Fri & Sat; ⛴ 1/2/5/13/17 Nieuwezijds Kolk

NO SMOKING (MOSTLY)

Amsterdam banned smoking in all bars and restaurants in 2008. A particularly devoted lot, Dutch smokers at first stowed their packets of Drum tobacco and complied with the law. But two years on, there's been some backsliding. In some bars, people light up freely and sealed, employee-free 'smoking rooms', installed for the ban, sit empty. Coffeeshops occupy odd territory: smoking marijuana is legit – but for a cigarette, technically, you have to step outside. Some places had stocked up on bongs and posted signs saying 'Pure marijuana only!' But it now appears the typical European tobacco-laced joint is again welcome indoors – as everyone looks the other way, in typically Dutch fashion. Only in Amsterdam, kids, only in Amsterdam.

This two-room bar has creaky wood floors and a tremendous selection of suds: more than 15 on tap and a couple of hundred in bottles from all over Europe. A crew of regulars makes this a haven in a touristy area.

IN 'T AEPJEN *Brown Cafe*
☎ 626 84 01; Zeedijk 1; ☺ 3pm-1am Mon-Thu, 3pm-3am Fri & Sat; ⓧ 4/9/16/24/25 Centraal Station
Candles burn even during the day at this super-*gezellig* (p160) bar in a 15th-century house, one of two remaining wooden buildings in the city. (The other's in the Begijnhof, p40.) Vintage jazz on the stereo enhances the time-warp feel. The name allegedly comes from the bar's role in the 16th and 17th centuries as a crash pad for sailors from the Far East,

who often toted *aapjes* (monkeys) with them.

KADINSKY *Coffeeshop*
☎ 624 70 23; Rosmarijnsteeg 9; ☺ 10am-1am; ⓧ 1/2/5 Spui
On the surface this could be an actual *coffee* shop – there's no trace of hippy grunge, just sleek minimalist furniture, cool electronica in the background, and good java and hot chocolate. Three levels offer various cosy nooks. Two much smaller branches are at Lange-brugsteeg 7a and Zoutsteeg 14.

LATEI *Cafe*
☎ 625 74 85; Zeedijk 143; ☺ 8am-6pm Mon-Wed, 8am-10pm Thu & Fri, 9am-10pm Sat, 11am-6pm Sun; ⓧ 4/9/16/24/25 Dam; Ⓥ ♿
Don't worry, the cool staff at this tiny cafe won't sell the Formica-top

table out from under you – though it, and every other piece of mod decor here, is for sale. A steady stream of neighbourhood residents pops in for *koffie verkeerd* (milky coffee).

SCHUIM *Bar*
☎ 638 93 57; Spuistraat 189; ⏰ 11am-1am Mon-Thu, 11am-3am Fri & Sat, 1pm-1am Sun; 🚊 1/2/5/14 Paleisstraat

Schuim means 'foam' and this arty bar doles it out – on the tops of beers – at a rapid rate. There's usually a substantial crowd here: grab a seat and watch artists, professionals and general street oddities mingle.

'T MANDJE
Gay & Lesbian, Brown Cafe
☎ 622 53 75; Zeedijk 63; 🚊 4/9/16/24/25 Centraal Station

Amsterdam's – and perhaps the world's – oldest gay bar opened in 1927, then shut in 1982, when the Zeedijk grew too seedy. But its trinket-covered interior was lovingly dusted every week until it reopened in 2008. The devoted bartenders can tell you stories about the bar's brassy lesbian founder, and there's live jazz and a retro DJ who spins 78s on a Victrola. One of the most *gezellig* places in the Centrum, gay or straight.

VRANKRIJK *Bar*
Spuistraat 216; ⏰ from 9pm; 🚊 1/2/5/14 Paleisstraat

Squatters keep it real at this grungy, graffiti-covered and very cheap bar, which functions as a social-support centre for Amsterdam's various subcultures. Monday is always Queer Night, Thursday is for punks and Saturday usually sees some sweaty dancing.

WYNAND FOCKINK
Tasting House
☎ 639 26 95; Pijlsteeg 31; ⏰ 3-9pm; 🚊 4/9/16/24/25 Dam

The crowd gets boisterous in this 1679 tasting room, despite the early closing time and the admonition over the door: 'Shh…the *jenever* is resting.' The distillery is also open for tours from 9am to 5pm weekdays and 1pm to 6pm Saturday.

PLAY

BITTERZOET *Live Music*
☎ 421 23 18; www.bitterzoet.com, in Dutch; Spuistraat 2; 🚊 1/2/5/13/17 Martelaarsgracht

This small but versatile live-music venue keeps a fresh attitude with a calendar that includes Afrobeat, Latin, hip hop and old-school jazz. We have received a couple of reports of a tourist-hostile attitude at the door, but this is not something we have noticed in person.

⭐ CASA ROSSO *Sex Show*
☎ 627 89 54; www.Janot.com; Oudezijds Achterburgwal 106-108; admission €30; ⏱ 8pm-2am Sun-Thu, 8pm-3am Fri & Sat; 🚋 4/9/16/24/25 Dam

It might be stretching it to describe a live sex show as 'classy', but this theatre is clean and comfortable and always packed with couples and hen's-night parties. We miss the penis fountain out front – look instead for the giant pink elephant sign.

⭐ CASABLANCA
Live Music, Theatre
☎ 625 56 85; www.casablanca -amsterdam.nl, in Dutch; Zeedijk 24; 🚋 4/9/16/24/25 Centraal Station

Split-personality Casablanca once had a hot reputation for jazz (combos still take the stage early in the week), but now it's better known as a karaoke madhouse on the weekends. Next door at No 26 is Casablanca Varieté, an intimate cabaret-style theatre where Dutch drag queens, magicians and more take the stage Tuesday to Sunday, for just a €5 cover charge.

⭐ WINSTON KINGDOM
Live Music
☎ 623 13 80; www.winston.nl; Warmoesstraat 131; 🚋 4/9/16/ 24/25 Dam

Something about being in a small space with a loud band makes people drink *a lot*. No matter what's on – from Brazilian DJs to Elvis Costello cover bands – the scene can get pretty wild in this grungy little club. Check the website for agenda details.

>JORDAAN & WESTERN CANALS

First dug in the 17th century, the Grachtengordel (Canal Belt) offered bigger lots for wealthy businessmen to live in the style they deserved – and it's still the city's best address. Many grand old mansions here are now offices, schools and exhibition space, but the wide, watery avenues retain a sedate, residential feel. (Mnemonic tip: Herengracht, Keizersgracht and Prinsengracht are in alphabetical order as you head out from the centre.) The single-block cross-streets that link them are livelier and packed with quirky shops and cafes – most famously in the Negen Straatjes (Nine Streets, p14) area south of Raadhuisstraat, but also to the north.

Due west of the canals is the Jordaan, a neighbourhood with working-class roots. Old-time residents are proud of their distinctive accent, their romantic music (*levenslied,* the tears-in-your-beer ballad style, flourishes here) and a checkered history that includes an 1886 brawl with the police that started with a greased-eel-pulling contest. The neighbourhood has weathered extreme gentrification, beginning in the early 20th century when tenements were razed up to the 1980s and it became the city's hot district, but it hasn't lost its tight-knit village feel. So while there's an olive-oil boutique and many art galleries, there are also secondhand clothing stores and lace curtains, even in the windows of generic 1980s rebuilds. With a charming small bar on nearly every corner, the Jordaan is a font of *gezelligheid* (p160).

Bordering both neighbourhoods on the north is Haarlemmerstraat and Haarlemmerdijk – one long, busy shopping street with a hipper edge, and lots of places to snack or relax over a drink.

JORDAAN & WESTERN CANALS

Please see over for map

JORDAAN & WESTERN CANALS

See City Centre
Map pp38–9

Het IJ

Van Diemenstraat

JORDAAN

Nassaukade

400 m

0.2 miles

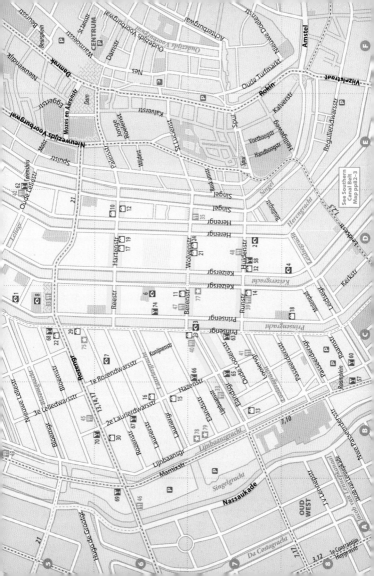

◉ SEE

◉ ANNE FRANK HUIS

☎ 556 71 05; www.annefrank
.org; Prinsengracht 267; adult/child
under 10yr/child 10-17yr €8.50/free/4;
⏱ 9am-9pm Sun-Fri, 9am-10pm Sat
mid-Mar–Jun, 9am-10pm Jul & Aug,
9am-7pm Sep–mid-Mar; 🚋 13/14/17
Westermarkt; ♿

The Anne Frank Huis (see also
p11), where the teenage diarist
hid with her family during WWII,
receives nearly a million visitors
a year. To skip the queue, buy
tickets online; the next best option
is to show up early or late, or on
a very drizzly day. The line moves
steadily, though, as it takes only
about 45 minutes to tour the
house and the adjacent exhibits.

◉ BIJBELS MUSEUM

☎ 624 24 36; www.bijbelsmuseum
.nl; Herengracht 366-368; admission
€8/4; ⏱ 10am-5pm Mon-Sat, 11am-5pm
Sun; 🚋 1/2/5 Spui

Not just a museum of Bibles, this
canal house trove is more like a
museum of the importance of the
Bible in 19th-century culture. It
contains musty mummies, hand-
carved models of the Tabernacle
and the Temple in Jerusalem, as
well as some antique Bibles. Near
the pretty garden, there's also a
display of biblical smells (nicer
than it sounds).

◉ HOUSEBOAT MUSEUM

☎ 427 07 50; www.houseboatmuseum
.nl; admission €3.50/2.75; ⏱ 11am-5pm
Tue-Sun Mar-Oct, 11am-5pm Fri-Sun
Nov-Feb, closed Jan; 🚋 13/14/17
Westermarkt

If you're curious how people live
on a *woonboot* (houseboat), then
check out the quarters on the *Hen-
drika Maria*, a former commercial
ship built in 1914. There's a short
video presentation on the varieties of houseboats, but the really
interesting part is just feeling an
apartment rock beneath your feet.
It's opposite Prinsengracht 296.

◉ HUIS MARSEILLE

☎ 531 89 89; www.huismarseille
.nl; Keizersgracht 401; admission €5/3;
⏱ 11am-6pm Tue-Sun; 🚋 1/2/5
Keizersgracht

Whether you prefer this contemporary photography museum or
FOAM (p81) depends largely on
what is showing. But the setting
here is lovelier, with exhibitions of
international work in five spacious
rooms complete with 18th-century
details, and a tiny summerhouse in
the garden. There's a terrific little
library too.

◉ KARTHUIZERHOF

Karthuizersstraat; admission free;
⏱ 8am-10pm; 🚋 3/10 Marnixplein

Amsterdam's generous public
housing system includes the

homes around this courtyard (similar to the Begijnhof, p40), one of the few of the city's 40-odd *hofjes* (Golden Age charity homes) that are open to visitors. This one was built in 1650.

NEDERLANDS INSTITUUT VOOR MEDIAKUNST

☎ 623 71 01; www.nimk.nl; Keizersgracht 264; admission €4.50/2.50; 11am-6pm Tue-Fri, 1-6pm Sat; 13/14/17 Westermarkt

Since the 1970s, the Netherlands Media Art Institute has amassed a collection of video and other multimedia work, including numerous pieces by onetime city resident Marina Abramović. This, along with new commissions, is installed in rotating exhibits in a warren of canal-house rooms. Expect to have your mind expanded at every turn.

STEDELIJK MUSEUM BUREAU AMSTERDAM

☎ 422 04 71; www.smba.nl; Rozenstraat 59; admission free; 11am-5pm Tue-Sun; 13/14/17 Westermarkt

While the Stedelijk Museum (p98) is undergoing its restoration, this is its only other permanent outlet. It doesn't display works from the Stedelijk collection, but instead mounts new works in installation, photography, design and new media.

GABLE STONES

Before street numbers were introduced in 1795, many Amsterdam homes were identified by a painted or carved stone plaque above the doorway. Beautiful examples of these gable stones are still in place particularly in the Jordaan, and salvaged ones have been installed outside Amsterdams Historisch Museum (p40) and in the Begijnhof (p40). Occupations are a frequent theme – tobacconists, skippers, even undertakers. Animals are also popular: the bar De Kat in de Wijngaert (p73) takes its name, The Cat in the Vineyard, from its gable stone. Modern buildings sometimes get a new old-style plaque – there's a particularly clever one at Lindengracht 55.

WESTERKERK

☎ 624 77 66; www.westerkerk.nl; Prinsengracht 281; admission free, tower €6; church 11am-3pm Mon-Fri Apr-Oct, also Sat Jul & Aug, tower 10am-6pm Mon-Sat Apr-Sep, to 8pm Jul & Aug; 13/14/17 Westermarkt

Though it's technically not in the Jordaan, this massive Protestant church, built in 1631, has become a symbol of the neighbourhood. Its 85m-high tower is the city's tallest. To be a true *jordaner*, it's said, you must be born within earshot of the Westerkerk's carillon bells and, according to church records, Rembrandt lies here, in an unmarked pauper's grave. Climbing the tower

NEIGHBOURHOODS

JORDAAN & WESTERN CANALS

Stop by for a bargain at the Noordermarkt (p67), held every Monday and Saturday

reveals a fine view, but it's not for the faint-hearted – there's a perceptible sway in windy weather.

🛍 SHOP

🛍 & KLEVERING *Housewares*
☎ 422 27 08; Haarlemmerstraat 8;
🚊 1/2/5/13/17 Martelaarsgracht
A branch of the nifty shop near Vondelpark (p99).

🛍 ANTONIA BY YVETTE *Footwear*
☎ 320 94 43; Herengracht 243;
🕐 Tue-Sat; 🚊 1/2/5/14 Paleisstraat
A wonderland of footwear for men and women, which overflows into the building next door: stilettos,

boots, espadrilles and even house slippers, from an assortment of international brands.

🛍 BOEKIE WOEKIE *Books*
☎ 639 05 07; Berenstraat 16;
🕐 noon-6pm; 🚊 13/14/17 Westermarkt
Essentially an art gallery, except the works here are all books by artists, whether that means a self-published monograph or an illustrated story that's handcrafted right down to the paper.

🛍 BRILMUSEUM *Eyeglasses*
☎ 421 24 14; Gasthuismolensteeg 7;
🕐 noon-5.30pm Wed-Fri, noon-5pm Sat;
🚊 1/2/5/14 Paleisstraat

NEIGHBOURHOODS

JORDAAN & WESTERN CANALS

The Museum of Spectacles displays 700 years' worth of glasses and sells unworn vintage frames, for anyone who wants to look like Jackie O or Buddy Holly.

🏠 DE LOOIER *Antiques*
☎ 624 90 38; Elandsgracht 109;
🕐 11am-5pm Sat-Thu; 🚊 7/10/17 Elandsgracht
Anyone with an affinity for odd antiques and bric-a-brac may enter this knick-knack minimall and never come out. You're just as likely to find 1940s silk dresses as you are 1970s Swedish porn.

🏠 DE WITTE TANDEN WINKEL *Speciality Shop*
☎ 623 34 43; Runstraat 5; 🕐 Mon-Sat; 🚊 1/2/5 Spui
We love shops that are obsessed, and the 'White-Teeth Shop' certainly is – with dental hygiene. Pop in here for toothbrushes, toothpastes from around the world and brushing accessories you never knew you needed.

🏠 ENGLISH BOOKSHOP *Books*
☎ 626 42 30; Lauriergracht 71;
🕐 Tue-Sat; 🚊 7/10/17 Elandsgracht
Stocked with the best range of Dutch literature and books on Amsterdam available in English, this is a great place to browse. It also features an excellent contemporary fiction section and a basement full of children's books.

🏠 EVA DAMAVE *Clothing*
☎ 627 73 25; 2e Laurierdwarsstraat 51c;
🕐 noon-6pm Wed-Sat; 🚊 10/13/14/17 Marnixstraat
Wool is the medium for this designer, who weaves punchy sweaters, shawls and dresses. Some of the patchwork styles are a bit too 'Cosby sweater' for our tastes, but the striped pieces are subtle and beautiful, and usually one-of-a-kind.

🏠 EXOTA *Clothing*
☎ 623 18 88; Hartenstraat 13;
🕐 10am-6pm Mon-Sat, noon-5pm Sun; 🚊 13/14/17 Westermarkt
A relatively inexpensive clothing shop in the Negen Straatjes, this is a great place to get the consummate Amsterdam woman's look: a frilly, delicate dress to wear over jeans in cooler weather. The house brand, King Louie, has a sweet retro sensibility, and there's some spunky menswear too. More women's and some kids' clothing is across the street at No 10.

🏠 FROZEN FOUNTAIN *Design*
☎ 622 93 75; Prinsengracht 645;
🚊 1/2/5 Prinsengracht
These two canal houses are crammed full of the cleverest, coolest home design you're likely to come across, most of it Dutch. You can spend thousands on a curlicue radiator, but there is a variety of

more accessible items, such as clever takes on Dutch bar towels.

☐ HESTER VAN EEGHEN
Footwear

☎ 626 92 11; Hartenstraat 1;
🕒 Tue-Sat; 🚊 13/14/17 Westermarkt

For her transfixing footwear, Van Eeghen applies bright solid colours to classic shapes – apple-green ankle boots, curvaceous red-and-pink pumps. Her handbags and wallets, just down the street at No 37, are just as attention grabbing.

☐ HET OUD-HOLLANDSCH SNOEPWINKELTJE
Food & Drink

☎ 420 73 90; 2e Egelantiersdwarsstraat 2; 🚊 3/10 Marnixplein

Look out for stampeding children before you reach for the door at this tiny corner shop filled floor to ceiling with sweets (and more than just liquorice), most sold in bulk from big glass jars.

☐ HJ VAN DE KERKHOF
Speciality Shop

☎ 623 46 66; Wolvenstraat 9-11;
🚊 13/14/17 Westermarkt

One of the Negen Straatje's most delightful old-fashioned stores, Kerkhof deals exclusively in passementerie: lace ribbon, rickrack, silk cord, curtain tassels. Surely *something* you own needs a little trim?

DROP IT LIKE IT'S HOT

The Dutch love their lollies, the most famous of which is *drop*, the word for all varieties of liquorice. It may be gummy-soft or tough as leather, shaped like coins or miniature cars, but the most important distinction is between *zoete* (sweet) and *zoute* (salty, also called *salmiak*). The latter is often an alarming surprise, even for avowed fans of the black stuff. But with such a range of textures and additional flavours – mint, honey, laurel – even liquorice-sceptics might be converted. Het Oud-Hollandsch Snoepwinkeltje (left) is a good place to do a taste test.

☐ KITSCH KITCHEN
Housewares

☎ 428 49 69; Rozengracht 8-12;
🚊 13/14/17 Westermarkt

No wonder this shop is so popular in cloudy Amsterdam: everywhere you lay your eyes is vibrant colour. Mexican flower-print vinyl sheeting is transformed into everything from bibs to bike bags, and there's also aluminium Thai soup bowls, groovy melamine plates and plenty more to liven up your home.

☐ LA SAVONNERIE
Perfume & Cosmetics

☎ 428 11 39; Prinsengracht 294;
🕒 Mon-Sat; 🚊 13/14/17 Westermarkt

Aromatic La Savonnerie is stocked with wonderful soaps from around the world, from Aleppo to Belgium. But the real star is the rainbowlike display of 80 or so soaps made in-house, with beautiful natural scents.

🏠 LAURA DOLS *Clothing*
☎ 624 90 66; Wolvenstraat 7;
🚋 13/14/17 Westermarkt
Some of the finest vintage clothing in the Netherlands – head here if you like your retro style glamorous, not campy. A shop across the street (No 6) handles the overflow, plus a line of home linens made from old-fashioned Dutch farm textiles.

🏠 MARLIES DEKKERS *Clothing*
☎ 421 19 00; Berenstraat 18;
🚋 13/14/17 Westermarkt
A branch of the Dutch lingerie queen (see p100).

🏠 MECHANISCH SPEELGOED
Children's
☎ 638 16 80; Westerstraat 67; 🚋 3/10 Marnixplein
Lure kids into further city exploring with a visit to this nostalgic toy shop that delights young and old. As the sign says, mechanical playthings are a speciality, whether intricate construction sets or wind-up tin figures.

🏠 MONO *Clothing*
☎ 421 50 78; Haarlemmerstraat 16;
🕐 10.30am-6pm Mon-Sat, noon-5pm Sun; 🚋 1/2/5/13/17 Martelaarsgracht

The owners of this little shop got their start at the Waterlooplein, selling sturdy canvas bags in groovy prints. It sounds like a contradiction in terms, but they even design very cool bumbags.

🏠 NOORDERMARKT
Clothing, Food & Drink
🕐 8am-1pm Mon, 9am-3pm Sat;
🚋 3 Nieuwe Willemsstraat
The square in front of the Noorderkerk hosts two markets: on Monday mornings, it's a trove of second-hand clothing (great rummage piles) and assorted antique trinkets, and on Saturdays, most (but not all) of the clothing stalls are replaced by gorgeous produce and cheese from growers around Amsterdam.

🏠 PAPABUBBLE *Food & Drink*
☎ 626 26 62; Haarlemmerdijk 70;
🕐 Mon-Sat; 🚋 3 Haarlemmerplein
This hip lolly shop looks more like a gallery. Pull up a cushion and perch on the stairs to watch the mesmerising process of transforming sugar into gemlike sweets with flavours like pomelo and lavender.

🏠 SHIRDAK
Clothing, Housewares
☎ 626 68 00; Prinsengracht 192;
🕐 11am-5.30pm Mon-Fri, 10am-5pm Sat; 🚋 13/14/17 Westermarkt
Wooden clogs not for you? Pick up a pair of beautiful soft felt ones

here, complete with whimsically curled toes. It also stocks felt clothing and blankets, as well as African, Chinese and Central Asian textiles.

SPRMRKT *Clothing, Design*
☎ 330 56 01; Rozengracht 191-193; 🚊 10/13/14/17 Marnixstraat

Whether you want a supertight pair of Acne jeans, a vintage Thor Larsen Pod chair or the latest copy of *Butt* magazine, it's at this industrial-feeling concept store, a major player in Amsterdam's fashion scene.

TYPIQUE *Stationery*
☎ 622 21 46; Haarlemmerdijk 123; 🚊 3 Haarlemmerplein

You probably don't have time to order custom letterhead from this old-fashioned printer, but you can pick up distinctive Amsterdam-theme greeting cards and other fine paper goods.

VAN RAVENSTEIN *Clothing*
☎ 639 00 67; Keizersgracht 359; 🕐 1-6pm Mon, 11am-6pm Tue, Wed & Fri, 11am-7pm Thu, 10.30am-5.30pm Sat; 🚊 1/2/5 Spui

The shop itself is minimalist, but all the better to show off all the big names in Dutch and Flemish fashion, such as Viktor & Rolf and Dries Van Noten – but then who can resist a little Givenchy on the side?

🍴 EAT

🍴 BALTHAZAR'S KEUKEN
Mediterranean €€
☎ 420 21 14; Elandsgracht 108; 🕐 6-11pm Wed-Fri; 🚊 7/10/17 Elandsgracht

This restaurant offers a fixed-price, three-course menu that changes weekly. With an open kitchen and only a few tables, it feels like eating at someone's house. It's only open three days a week so make sure you book ahead.

🍴 BORDEWIJK *French* €€€
☎ 624 38 99; Noordermarkt 7; 🕐 dinner Tue-Sun; 🚊 3 Nieuwe Willemsstraat

The chef at Bordewijk, one of the city's best French restaurants, is confident enough in his stellar food – rustic pâté, marrow bones, garlicky *bourride* – that he doesn't need to dress up the spare dining room with chandeliers or velvet banquettes. In summer, there are tables on the canal.

🍴 BUFFET VAN ODETTE
Cafe €
☎ 423 60 34; Herengracht 309; 🕐 8.30am-4.30pm Mon & Wed-Fri, 10am-5.30pm Sat & Sun; 🚊 1/2/5 Spui; Ⓥ ♿

It's hard to get a seat in this tiny place on the weekend – it's packed with customers noshing on fat meatloaf sandwiches and omelettes with truffle cheese. Stay for sweets too: the sticky toffee and carrot cakes are delicious.

🍴 CAULILS *Delicatessen* €
☎ 412 00 27; Haarlemmerstraat 115; 🕑 noon-7pm Mon-Fri, 10am-6pm Sat; 🚊 1/2/5/13/17 Martelaarsgracht

Compose a decadent picnic for Westerpark (p78) at this French deli – there's even a handy €20 'picknickpakket'. Just one of several great takeout options on this street.

🍴 DE BELHAMEL *French* €€
☎ 622 10 95; Brouwersgracht 60; 🕑 lunch & dinner; 🚊 1/2/5/13/17 Martelaarsgracht; **V**

A beautiful restaurant on a beautiful canal: the gorgeous art nouveau dining room takes on an almost palpable glow in the evenings. The food, while not quite as memorable as the scenery, does some neat hopping between French, Italian and Dutch, with excellent seafood.

🍴 DE BOLHOED
Vegetarian €€
☎ 626 18 03; Prinsengracht 60-62; 🕑 lunch & dinner; 🚊 13/14/17 Westermarkt; **V** 🚼

An old-school vegetarian eatery, De Bolhoed has been dishing up generous helpings of Italian, Mexican and Middle Eastern dishes to Amsterdammers for

decades. Arrive early for the vegan special.

🍴 DE KAASKAMER
Delicatessen €
☎ 623 34 83; Runstraat 7; 🚊 1/2/5 Spui

This wonderful cheese shop is the best in town for Dutch varieties, and also stocks olives, tapenades, salads and other picnic ingredients. You try before you buy, and they're happy to make up cheese baskets to take home.

🍴 DIVAN *Turkish* €€
☎ 626 82 39; Elandsgracht 14; 🕑 5-11pm; 🚊 13/14/17 Westermarkt; **V** 🚼

Though it looks like a standard brown cafe, this great little restaurant is one of Amsterdam's best Turkish restaurants, with exceptionally sweet service. Order some *meze* (mixed starters) and don't miss out on the lamb as a main course.

🍴 FESTINA LENTE
Cafe €€
☎ 638 14 12; Looiersgracht 40b; noon-1am Sun & Mon, 10.30am-1am Tue-Thu, 10.30am-3am Fri & Sat; 🚊 7/10/17 Elandsgracht; 🚼 **V**

This neighbourhood hangout is typical Jordaan *gezelligheid*, packed with regulars snacking on small-portion Mediterranean dishes and big sandwiches named after famous writers.

🍴 FOODISM
International   €€

☎ 627 64 24; Oude Leliestraat 8;
🕙 noon-6pm Mon & Tue, noon-10pm
Wed-Sat, 1-6pm Sun; 🚊 1/2/5/13/17
Raadhuisstraat; **V** ♿
A good all-day cafe with friendly
staff, Foodism serves up big
breakfasts, filling sandwiches (try
the goat's cheese and chorizo) and
hearty, handmade pastas. A good
selection of vegetarian dishes too.

🍴 LA PERLA *Italian*   €

2e Tuindwarsstraat 14; 🕙 5-10pm;
🚊 3/10 Marnixplein; ♿ ♿
Exceptionally good pizza, from the
crispy crust – a bit smoky from the
wood oven – up to the artisanal
Italian toppings, such as incredibly
creamy buffalo mozzarella and
delicate fennel sausage. Limited
seating; takeaway possible.

🍴 LOS PILONES
Mexican   €€

☎ 620 03 23; 1e Anjeliersdwarsstraat
6; 🕙 4-11.30pm Tue-Sun; 🚊 3/10
Marnixplein; **V** ♿
A branch of the Mexican place on
Kerkstraat (p88).

🍴 MERCAN *Turkish*   €

☎ 638 01 65; Rozengracht 148; 🕙 8am-
5pm; 🚊 10/13/14/17 Marnixstraat;
V ♿
This Turkish bakery is an excellent
pit stop for a *turkse pizza* – aka

lahmacun, a crispy flatbread that
is topped with spiced ground
meat, creamy yoghurt and hot
sauce and rolled up for easy
eating.

🍴 MOEDERS *Dutch*   €€

☎ 626 79 57; Rozengracht 251;
🕙 dinner; 🚊 10/13/14/17 Marnixstraat;
V ♿
'Mothers' is stocked with customers' own plates, flatware and photos of their mums, and the result is
a delightful hotchpotch. So is the
food, including seafood, Moroccan
dishes, a vegetarian frittata and
a *rijsttafel*-style presentation of
traditional Dutch dishes in many
small plates.

🍴 PANCAKES! *Dutch*   €

☎ 528 97 97; Berenstraat 38; 🕙 10am-
7pm; 🚊 13/14/17 Westermarkt; **V** ♿
A great place to sample Dutch
pancakes in an atmosphere free
of clogs and other kitsch – and
there are just as many locals here
as tourists. All the usual options,
plus daily creations like aubergine,
chicory and cheese, grace the
menu.

🍴 POMPADOUR
Bakery & Sweets   €

☎ 623 95 54; Huidenstraat 12;
🕙 10am-6pm Mon-Fri, 9am-5pm Sat,
noon-6pm Sun; 🚊 1/2/5 Spui
At this little gold-wallpapered
patisserie, join society ladies

Vic van Koningsbruggen
Amsterdam native, roving gourmet and freelance oysterman at 't Mandje (p56)

Why do you sell oysters so cheaply? I want to make a difference. People should taste Zeeland oysters – the best in the world. **Affordable eats** La Place at the library (p136) has an amazing view – take your camera. You can eat a full, healthy meal for less than €10. And the pie is really something – I always ask for a rude amount of whipped cream. **Asian treat** Nam Kee (p50, p129) for Chinese. Singapore noodles, with shrimp, beef, tofu, egg – they're the best. **'Typically Dutch' restaurants** As a Dutchman, I always compare prices. These places aren't worth it for me. I'm better off with 'Restaurant FEBO' (p88). **A good bar** Lived-in. Good staff, but they don't need to be friendly. And no music. **Best brews** When I worked at In de Wildeman (p54), I'd call out 'warm beer, lousy service'. And 't Arendsnest (p76) is excellent for Dutch beer.

After perusing the Noordermarkt (p67), settle down for an afternoon pastry or cake

sipping top-notch tea and nibbling at the Frenchiest cakes in town. Pompadour's handmade chocolates are tasty too, and you can get them to go.

🍴 SEMHAR *Ethiopian*   €€

☎ 638 16 34; Marnixstraat 259-261; 🕔 4-10pm Tue-Sun; 🚊 10 Bloemgracht; Ⓥ 🔖

Yohannes gives his customers a warm welcome, and he's a fanatic about the quality of his *injera* bread – all the better to sop up richly spiced stews and vegetable combos. We always skip the menu and just ask for a mixed platter.

🍴 SPANJER EN VAN TWIST
Cafe   €€

☎ 639 01 09; Leliegracht 60; 🕔 10am-1am; 🚊 13/14/17 Westermarkt; 🔖

Just north of Anne Frank Huis, Spanjer en Van Twist's tables on Leliegracht are great for watching the boats cruise by. The eclectic lunch and dinner menu is perfectly good, but it's a really great place for an afternoon pastry or cake.

🍴 STOUT *Cafe*   €€

☎ 616 36 64; Haarlemmerstraat 73; 🕔 10am-11pm Mon-Sat, noon-11pm Sun; 🚊 1/2/5/13/17 Martelaarsgracht; Ⓥ

A slick crowd congregates to read design magazines and share fusion dishes, such as carrot and coriander soup with spicy tempeh, Thai chicken burger with kimchi, and fruit shakes. Fitting for the name (*stout* means 'naughty' in Dutch), flirting seems to be a primary activity here.

UNLIMITED DELICIOUS
Bakery & Sweets €
☎ 622 48 29; Haarlemmerstraat 122;
⌚ Mon-Sat; 🚊 1/2/5/13/17
Martelaarsgracht

It's certainly tempting to dive into the gorgeous, sculptural cakes and tarts, but don't fill up before you get to the home-made chocolates. The fruit-chocolate combos are intense. You can either sit down and enjoy your selections with a coffee, or pack it all up to take away.

WIL GRAANSTRA FRITESHUIS *Fast Food* €
☎ 624 40 71; Westermarkt 11;
⌚ 11am-6pm; 🚊 13/14/17
Westermarkt; ♿ Ⓥ ☗

This little stall near Anne Frank Huis has been serving up fries with mayo since 1956. They're an almost eerie shade of gold, and delectably light and crispy.

WINKEL *Cafe* €
☎ 623 02 23; Noordermarkt 43;
⌚ breakfast, lunch & dinner;
🚊 3 Nieuwe Willemsstraat; ☗

This sprawling space serves meals, but most people come here just for its tall, cakey apple pie. You'd best not get a hankering for it on market days (Mondays and Saturdays), as there's almost always a queue out the door.

🍸 DRINK

🍸 BARNEY'S *Coffeeshop*
☎ 427 94 69; Haarlemmerstraat 102;
⌚ 7am-8pm; 🚊 1/2/5/13/17
Martelaarsgracht

Decades ago, Barney's got famous on bargain breakfasts all day, along with marijuana. In recent years, the weed has vastly improved, but breakfasts are now across the street in the smoke-friendly, somewhat slick Barney's Uptown. Other, cheaper wake-and-bake options are available along the same block.

🍸 DE KAT IN DE WIJNGAERT *Brown Cafe*
☎ 620 45 54; Lindengracht 160;
🚊 3 Nieuwe Willemsstraat

Rivalling 't Smalle (p77) for overwhelming *gezelligheid,* this gorgeous bar is the kind of place where one beer soon turns to half a dozen – maybe it's the bad influence of the old-guard arts types who hang out here. At least you can soak it all up with what many people vote as the best *tosti* (toasted sandwich) in town.

▼ DE KOE *Bar*
☎ 625 44 82; Marnixstraat 381;
🚊 7/10 Raamplein

With a pinball machine, darts, board games and good cheap meals on hand, you'll never get bored at 'the Cow', a casual spot not far from the Leidseplein.

▼ DE PELS *Brown Cafe*
☎ 622 90 37; Huidenstraat 25;
🚊 1/2/5 Spui

The action at this appealingly shabby *bruin café* is focused on reading the newspaper and drinking. It's also a Sunday morning breakfast favourite.

▼ DE TWEE ZWAANTJES
Brown Cafe
☎ 625 27 29; Prinsengracht 114;
🚊 13/14/17 Westermarkt

At this bar, crooners with big hair and ruffled shirts belt out nostalgic anthems with accordion accompaniment. Come here if you're sick of trendy lounges, and sing along if you can: *Oh Amsterdam, wat ben je mooi…* ('Oh Amsterdam, how beautiful you are… '). In summer, karaoke replaces the pros.

▼ DE ZOTTE *Beer Bar*
☎ 626 86 94; Raamstraat 29; 🚊 7/10 Raamplein

If you can't make up your mind in this Belgian beer bar, start with the weekly special. Those Trappist monks can brew some deadly ones so you might want to line your stomach with a hearty cheese plate or steak – the kitchen's open between 6.30pm and 9pm.

▼ FINCH *Cafe*
☎ 626 24 61; Noordermarkt 5;
🕑 9am-1am Sun-Thu, 9am-3am Fri & Sat; 🚊 3 Nieuwe Willemsstraat

This funky cafe-lounge is one of the major hangouts for more stylish Jordaan residents. When equally cool Proust bar next door also gets going, the place just hums.

▼ GREY AREA *Coffeeshop*
☎ 420 43 01; Oude Leliestraat 2;
🕑 noon-8pm; 🚊 1/2/5/13/17 Raadhuisstraat

Owned by a couple of guys from the US, this tiny shop plastered with band and skateboard stickers doles out specialities like 'Double Bubble-Gum' to regular customers. It also keeps up the American tradition of coffee refills (it's organic).

▼ LA TERTULIA *Coffeeshop*
☎ 623 85 03; Prinsengracht 312;
🕑 11am-7pm Tue-Sat; 🚊 7/10/17 Elandsgracht

This plant-filled canalside spot is great for a sunny-day smoke. The weed selection is limited, so you might want to just treat it as a stoner-friendly cafe, complete with delicious juices, herbal teas and toasted sandwiches.

ROKERIJ *Coffeeshop*
☎ 623 03 98; Elandsgracht 53;
🕐 10am-1am; 🚊 7/10/17 Elandsgracht
An all-Indian-theme branch of the Leidseplein operation (p91). Yet another, at Singel 8, has an even trippier interior.

SAAREIN II *Gay & Lesbian*
☎ 623 49 01; Elandsstraat 119; 🕐 4pm-1am Tue-Thu & Sun, 4pm-2am Fri, noon-2am Sat; 🚊 7/10/17 Elandsgracht
Saarein was a focal point for the feminist movement in the 1970s and had a women-only policy. It has since relaxed a bit, and bills itself as a 'mixed gay cafe', though the crowd still skews female.

SANEMENTERENG *Coffeeshop*
☎ 624 19 07; 2e Laurierdwarsstraat 44;
🚊 10/13/14/17 Marnixstraat

One minute you're picking through secondhand trinkets on the pavement outside. Next minute you're buying a chipped delftware plate and a gram of out-door-grown ganja, and grooving to the strains of 'Legalise It'. Hours can be erratic, but it usually opens around 2pm.

SIMON LÉVELT *Cafe*
☎ 624 08 23; Prinsengracht 180;
🕐 10am-6pm Mon-Fri, 10am-5pm Sat, 1-5pm Sun; 🚊 13/14/17 Westermarkt
For more than two centuries, Lévelt has been selling tea and coffee in the Netherlands. This is its original shopfront, and it has a beautiful little garden out the back.

SOUND GARDEN *Bar*
☎ 620 28 53; Marnixstraat 164-66;
🚊 10/13/14/17 Marnixstraat
The grunge-era name is no coincidence – the soundtrack at

GO WEST?
Beyond the Jordaan, Amsterdam West fosters some grassroots cool. The neighbourhood clubhouse is **De Nieuwe Anita** (☎ 064 150 35 12; www.denieuweanita.nl, in Dutch; Frederik Hendrikstraat 111; 🚊 3 Hugo de Grootplein), an intimate living-roomlike art lounge, while bare-bones **Club 8** (☎ 685 17 03; www.club-8.nl, in Dutch; Admiraal de Ruijterweg 56b; 🚊 12/13/14 Admiraal de Ruijterweg) hosts dance parties and art shows. Also check out legalised squat **Zaal 100** (☎ 688 01 27; www.zaal100.nl, in Dutch; De Wittenstraat 100; 🚊 10 De Wittenkade) for its Tuesday improvised jam session, and multicultural arts space **Podium Mozaïek** (☎ 580 03 80; www.podiummozaiek.nl, in Dutch; Bos en Lommerweg 191; 🚊 12/14 Bos en Lommerweg).

this roomy, ramshackle bar tends towards ragged indie rock. But there is a genuine garden – a large terrace out back on the canal. Pinball and cheap drinks are bonuses.

STRUIK *Bar & Cafe*
☎ 625 48 63; Rozengracht 160; 🚊 10/13/14/17 Marnixstraat
If you prefer your beer with a background of hip hop, breakbeats and soul, come to this laid-back corner cafe, which does good food (rockin' roti on Tuesdays, and a hangover brunch on Sundays) then segues into drinking and chatting along to an old-school playlist or a DJ on weekends.

'T ARENDSNEST *Beer Bar*
☎ 421 20 57; Herengracht 90; ⏰ 4pm-midnight Sun-Thu, 4pm-2am Fri & Sat; 🚊 1/2/5/13/17 Nieuwezijds Kolk
This cosy bar stocks only Dutch beers, which are often over-shadowed by Belgian ones. The bartenders are evangelistic about the options from more than 50 breweries – ask for their expert recommendations!

Patrons enjoying a splash of Amsterdam's fickle sunshine at Finch (p74)

'T SMALLE *Brown Cafe*
☎ 623 96 17; Egelantiersgracht 12;
🕐 10am-1am; 🚊 13/14/17
Westermarkt

There's no more convivial spot than this canalside terrace on a sunny day and the 18th-century interior is perfect in winter. Proof of its powerful *gezelligheid,* it manages to remain a lively local bar even while being gushed over in almost every guidebook in print.

VESPER *Bar*
☎ 062 294 41 63; Vinkenstraat 57;
🕐 5pm-1am Tue-Thu, 5pm-3am Fri, 4pm-3am Sat; 🚊 3 Haarlemmerplein

A friendly corner bar that just happens to have some of the best cocktails in Amsterdam, Vesper doesn't take itself too seriously: bartender Isaac from *The Love Boat* grins from the menu. Try a tequila tasting flight, or ask the staff to whip up something to suit your mood. Beer and wine drinkers also have good choices.

VYNE *Wine Bar*
☎ 344 64 08; Prinsengracht 411;
🕐 6pm-midnight Mon-Thu, 5pm-1am Fri & Sat, 5-10pm Sun; 🚊 13/14/17 Westermarkt; ♿ Ⓥ

This sleek space is one of the few wine bars in town. It does a particularly great job of pairing snacks with every variety of vino,

and we especially recommend the Love Bites – fancy-flavoured, all-vegetarian *bitterballen* (minicroquettes).

PLAY

COC AMSTERDAM
Gay & Lesbian
☎ 626 30 87; www.cocamsterdam.nl, in Dutch; Rozenstraat 14; 🚊 13/14/17 Westermarkt

HQ of the national gay and lesbian organisation holds weekly parties and other get-togethers.

DECO SAUNA *Sauna*
☎ 623 82 15; Herengracht 115; admission €19.50; 🕐 noon-11pm Mon & Wed-Sat, 3-11pm Tue, 1-8pm Sun; 🚊 1/2/5/13/17 Nieuwezijds Kolk

Steam yourself in art deco splendour – this beautiful sauna is a wonderful way to warm up on a grey afternoon. Note that it's all-nude and unisex, even in the dressing rooms.

FELIX MERITIS
Arts Centre
☎ 626 23 21; www.felixmeritis.nl; Keizersgracht 324; 🕐 box office 9am-7pm Mon-Fri; 🚊 13/14/17 Westermarkt; ♿

This wonderful arts and culture space, established in 1777, occasionally hosts experimental European theatre, along with innovative music, dance, and

WORTH THE TRIP

Just to the north of the Jordaan, the Westelijke Eilanden (Western Islands) were originally home to shipworks and the West India Trading Company warehouses. The district
is a world unto itself, cut through with canals and linked with small drawbridges. It's
home to artists' studios and foodie favourite **Marius** (☎ 422 78 80; Barentszstraat 243;
✌ dinner Tue-Sat; 🚊 3 Zoutkeetsgracht) – Chef Kees is an alumnus of California's
Chez Panisse.

To the west of the islands, **Het Schip** (☎ 418 28 85; www.hetschip.nl; Spaarn-
dammerplantsoen 140; adult/child/concession €5/2/2.75; ✌ 1-5pm Wed-Sun; 🚊 22
Zaanstraat) is one of the most fabulous housing projects you'll ever see. The pinnacle –
almost literally: check out that tower! – of Amsterdam School style (see boxed text, p106),
it now hosts a small museum in three parts: you can poke around the delightful old post
office, walk through an apartment and enjoy a drink in the teahouse.

From Het Schip, you can walk back southeast along the train tracks and cut through
a small underpass to **Westerpark**. This sprawling patch of green is a bit of a hipster
hangout, perhaps because it's adjacent to **Westergasfabriek** (☎ 586 07 10; www
.westergasfabriek.nl; Haarlemmerweg 8-10; 🚊 3 Haarlemmerplein), a former gasworks
that has been transformed into an edgy cultural park, filled with bars, concert halls and
restaurants.

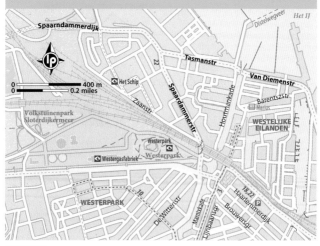

lectures and readings. The cafe here, with its huge open windows, is particularly great.

⭐ MALOE MELO *Live Music*

☎ 420 45 92; www.maloemelo.nl; **Lijnbaansgracht 163;** ⏲ **9pm-3am Sun-Thu, 9pm-4am Fri & Sat;** 🚊 **7/10/17 Elandsgracht**

Home to Amsterdam's blues scene, this dingy venue is rowdy and casual, and often adds blue-grass and soul to the calendar. If nothing appeals here, goth and new-wave **Korsakoff** (☎ 625 78 54;

Lijnbaansgracht 161), next door, might do.

⭐ MOVIES *Cinema*

☎ **638 60 16; www.themovies.nl, in Dutch; Haarlemmerdijk 161; admission €8.50/7.50;** ⏲ **1.30pm-midnight;** 🚊 **3 Haarlemmerplein**

Indie features (often in English) rule at this beautiful art deco cinema. The sweet Wild Kitchen restaurant offers a reasonable package of a two-course meal and movie ticket for €28.

>SOUTHERN CANAL BELT

The southern stretch of the Grachtengordel, completed when the city was wallowing in cash at the end of the 17th century, is even ritzier than the western area. Yet even the double-wide mansions on the so-called Gouden Bocht (Golden Bend) – Herengracht between Leidsestraat and Vijzelstraat – are not gaudy: the various styles all blend into a seamless whole. The interiors of the homes are grand too – at least judging from the shops along Nieuwe Spiegelstraat, Amsterdam's address for museum-quality antiques.

At either end of the neighbourhood, old money gives way to neon glitz in the Leidseplein and Rembrandtplein. Feeding into the Leidseplein is the shopping street of Leidsestraat, packed with a disproportionately large number of shoe shops and fast-food outlets. South of Rembrandtplein, the Utrechtsestraat is a chic strip of boutiques and excellent restaurants.

SOUTHERN CANAL BELT

◎ SEE
Bloemenmarkt 1 D2
FOAM 2 D3
Greenbox Museum 3 A3
Hermitage
    Amsterdam 4 G2
Het Kattenkabinet 5 D2
Mediamatic Bank 6 D3
Museum Van Loon 7 D3
Museum
    Willet-Holthuysen 8 F2
Stadsarchief 9 D3
Tassenmuseum
    Hendrikje 10 E3
Tuschinskitheater 11 E2

◎ SHOP
BeBob Design 12 F4
Concerto 13 F3
Cora Kemperman 14 B3
Eduard Kramer 15 C4
Fred de la
    Bretonière 16 F3
Lambiek 17 C3

TinkerBell 18 C4
Young Designers
    United 19 B2

🍴 EAT
Burger Bar 20 E2
Coffee & Jazz 21 F4
De Carrousel 22 D6
FEBO 23 E2
FEBO 24 B3
Los Pilones 25 B3
Maoz 26 D2
Maoz 27 B3
Pata Negra 28 F4
Taste of Culture 29 B4
Tempo Doeloe 30 F3
Van Dobben 31 E2
Walem 32 B2
Wok to Walk 33 B3

🍷 DRINK
Barney's Lounge 34 E3
Bo Cinq 35 B3
Café Américain 36 A3

Café Schiller 37 E2
De Huyschkaemer 38 F4
De Koffie Salon 39 F4
Door 74 ....40 D2
Rokerij 41 B3
Rokerij 42 E2
Vivelavie 43 F2
Weber 44 A3

⭐ PLAY
Air 45 F2
Boom Chicago 46 A3
Escape 47 E2
Jazz Café Alto 48 B3
Jimmy Woo 49 A3
Melkweg 50 A3
Paradiso 51 B4
Stadsschouwburg 52 A3
Studio 80 ....53 E2
Sugar Factory 54 A3
TWSTd 55 D5
Uitburo 56 A3
Up 57 B3

Please see over for map

The Bloemenmarkt is an Amsterdam icon

 SEE

🔘 BLOEMENMARKT

Singel btwn Koningsplein & Muntplein; 🕑 **9am-5.30pm Mon-Sat, 11am-5.30pm Sun;** 🚋 **1/2/5 Koningsplein**

This canalside flower market has been here since the 1860s, when gardeners used to sail up the Amstel and sell from their boats. Many vendors sell more bulbs than cut flowers, so it's not the riot of colour you might have expected, but it's still a pretty place for a stroll, and perhaps to pick up a bouquet to brighten up your hotel room.

🔘 FOAM

Fotografiemuseum Amsterdam; ☎ **551 65 00; www.foam.nl; Keizersgracht 609; adult/under 12yr/student €8/free/5.50;** 🕑 **10am-6pm Sat-Wed, 10am-9pm Thu & Fri;** 🚋 **16/24/25 Keizersgracht**

Rotating work at this hyper-modernised canal-house space ranges from that of photography giants such as Richard Avedon to relative unknowns like Malick Sidibé, a Malian portraitist. The museum also prints an edgy magazine four times a year and hosts a variety of photographers' confabs.

🔘 GREENBOX MUSEUM

☎ **062 428 28 84; www.greenbox museum.com; Korte Leidsedwarsstraat 12; admission €5;** 🕑 **by appointment;** 🚋 **1/2/5/7/10 Leidseplein;** ♿

Obsessive Amsterdam at its best: at this fascinating collection of contemporary art from Saudi Arabia, you get a personal tour from the enthusiastic owner himself.

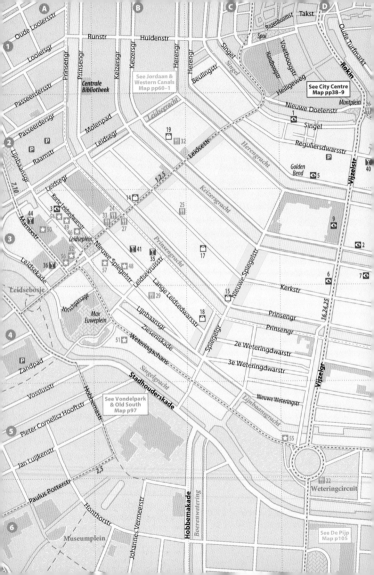

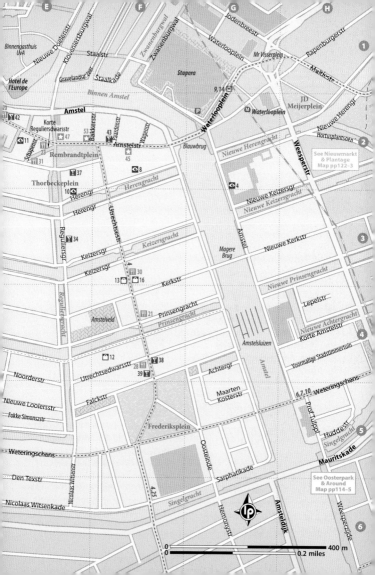

⊙ HERMITAGE AMSTERDAM

☎ 530 74 88; www.hermitage.nl; Amstel 51; admission €15/free; ⏲ 10am-5pm Thu-Tue, 10am-8pm Wed; 🚊 9/14 Waterlooplein

Given Peter the Great's admiration for Golden Age Amsterdam, this satellite of the Russian Hermitage Museum makes perfect sense. It occupies the vast Amstelhof, an old-age home since the 17th century, and displays one-off exhibits, from Matisse to treasures from the ancient world, many of which have rarely been shown in public before. There's a free tour in English on Sundays at 2pm.

⊙ HET KATTENKABINET

☎ 626 53 78; www.kattenkabinet.nl; Herengracht 497; admission €5/2.50; ⏲ 10am-4pm Mon-Fri, noon-5pm Sat & Sun; 🚊 4/16/24/25 Keizersgracht

Eccentric Amsterdam caters to fans of felines: this creaky old canal house is full of cat-related art by the likes of Toulouse-Lautrec and Picasso as well as odd ephemera, including an actual Egyptian mummy. A few happy live cats lounge around on the window seats.

⊙ MEDIAMATIC BANK

☎ 638 99 01; www.mediamatic.net; Vijzelstraat 68; ⏲ 1-9pm Mon-Fri, 1-6pm Sat & Sun; 🚊 16/24/25 Keizersgracht

Step into this repurposed bank office to see art that's both bizarre and hilarious (Jerry Springer inspired one recent installation). Just as often, there are graffiti workshops, conceptual dinners and inspiring talks going on.

⊙ MUSEUM VAN LOON

☎ 624 52 55; www.museumvanloon .nl; Keizersgracht 672; admission €7/5; ⏲ 11am-5pm Wed-Mon; 🚊 16/24/25 Keizersgracht

Arguably the best of the canal-house museums, this 1672 mansion was first home to painter Ferdinand Bol; in the 19th century, the Van Loon family (descendants of Willem van Loon, cofounder of the Dutch East India Company) moved in. Start in the basement with the introductory video, in which a family member tells anecdotes about visiting his grandmother in the house, then wander through the shadowy rooms adorned with rich wallpaper, worn carpets and well-used Louis XV furniture.

⊙ MUSEUM WILLET-HOLTHUYSEN

☎ 523 18 22; www.willetholthuysen .nl; Herengracht 605; admission €7/3.50; ⏲ 10am-5pm Mon-Fri, 11am-5pm Sat & Sun; 🚊 4/9/14 Rembrandtplein

This mansion has been a museum since 1895, when a wealthy widow gave the city her home and her husband's assorted treasures – furniture, paintings and loads of

18th-century china. It's a bit fussier than the Van Loon (left), but the *objets* are lovely.

◎ STADSARCHIEF
**Municipal Archives; ☎ 251 15 11; www
.stadsarchief.amsterdam.nl; Vijzelstraat 32; admission free, audio tour €4;
☉ 10am-5pm Tue-Fri, 11am-5pm Sat &
Sun; ▣ 16/24/25 Keizersgracht; ☦**
The Amsterdam archives occupy a monumental bank building which dates from 1923. When you step inside head to the left, to the enormous tiled basement vault and displays of archive gems such as the 1942 police report on the theft of Anne Frank's bike. A small cinema at the back shows vintage films about the city. Upstairs, a gallery space is dedicated to tem-porary exhibits (for a small entry fee), and there's a good bookshop. Free tours of the building run at 1pm from Tuesday to Friday and at 3pm on Saturday and Sunday.

◎ TASSENMUSEUM HENDRIKJE
**☎ 524 64 52; www.tassenmuseum.nl;
Herengracht 573; admission €7.50/4;
☉ 10am-5pm; ▣ 4/9/14
Rembrandtplein**
Dedicated entirely to handbags, this chic canal-house museum is surprisingly interesting even for nonfashionistas. However, the signage is not as thorough as it

could be and, In what seems like a major gap, there's no Birkin on display.

◎ TUSCHINSKITHEATER
**☎ 428 10 60; www.pathe.nl, in Dutch;
Reguliersbreestraat 26; admission
€10-11; ☉ noon-midnight; ▣ 4/9/14
Rembrandtplein**
Built in 1921, this fantastic theatre melds art deco and Amsterdam School architecture. Faithfully re-stored, the interior features a huge handmade carpet and a striking cupola that should never meet the gaze of someone on hallucino-gens. You'll have to endure a Hollywood blockbuster to eyeball the marvellous main hall, but then you can also peek at the Japanese Room upstairs. While you're here, note the Cineac building across the street – this austere functional-ist building was erected just over a decade later.

🛍 SHOP
🏠 BEBOB DESIGN *Design*
**☎ 624 57 63; Prinsengracht 764;
☉ noon-6pm Mon, 11am-6pm Thu-Sat;
▣ 4 Prinsengracht**
Those with a midcentury-modern chair fetish will be sated with Eames, Aalto and others at this secondhand design warehouse. Shipping can be arranged, but a George Nelson ball clock should fit nicely in your carry-on.

☐ CONCERTO Music

☎ 623 52 28; Utrechtsestraat 52-60; ⏱ 10am-6pm Mon-Wed, Fri & Sat, 10am-9pm Thu, noon-6pm Sun; 🚋 4 Keizersgracht

Spread over several buildings, this is the city's most engaging music store. Ideal for browsing, it has an eclectic (and often cheap) collection of new and second-hand records, CDs and DVDs, and good listening facilities.

☐ CORA KEMPERMAN Clothing

☎ 625 12 84; Leidsestraat 72; 🚋 1/2/5 Prinsengracht

No matter what the season, Amsterdam's Cora Kemperman's striking, ethnic-inspired collections are defined by natural fabrics, crushed and crinkled looks, and lots of layers, volume and shape.

☐ EDUARD KRAMER Antiques

☎ 626 11 16; Nieuwe Spiegelstraat 76; 🚋 16/24/25 Keizersgracht

Specialising in antique Dutch tiles, this tiny store is also crammed with lots of other interesting stuff – silver candlesticks, crystal decanters, jewellery and pocket watches.

☐ FRED DE LA BRETONIÈRE Footwear

☎ 626 96 27; Utrechtsestraat 77; ⏱ 1-6pm Mon, 10am-6pm Tue, Wed & Fri, 10am-9pm Thu, 10am-5pm Sat, 1-5pm Sun; 🚋 4 Keizersgracht

A branch of the sensible-yet-fun Dutch shoe shop (p45).

☐ LAMBIEK Books

☎ 626 75 43; Kerkstraat 132; ⏱ 11am-6pm Mon-Fri, 11am-5pm Sat, 1-5pm Sun; 🚋 16/24/25 Keizersgracht

Comics specialist Lambiek has been in operation since 1968, stocking an impressive range of underground comics and newspaper strips, along with classics such as Tintin and Asterix. A gallery displays new comix-inspired art.

☐ TINKERBELL Children's

☎ 625 88 30; Spiegelgracht 10; 🚋 7/10 Spiegelgracht

Kids are fascinated by the mechanical bear that blows bubbles outside this shop; inside, there's a great selection of wood toys, historical costumes and plush animals – no blinking lights or batteries here.

☐ YOUNG DESIGNERS UNITED Clothing

☎ 626 91 91; Keizersgracht 447; ⏱ 1-6pm Mon, 10am-6pm Tue-Sat; 🚋 1/2/5 Keizersgracht

This boutique showcases young Dutch designers, each displayed on its own rack. The range is huge, from abstract, asymmetrical sheaths to sexy, flower-bedecked frocks, all fairly well priced.

Dani Burguess
Bartender at Door 74 (p91)

Dutch 'style' This is a young, cosmopolitan city, but no one dresses up! And they're surprised when we take their coats here at the bar – that gesture isn't common. **Getting comfortable** Dutch people value *gezelligheid* – so slick lounges often don't succeed because they're not homey. De Pijp has the most *gezellig* pubs. **Nightlife** Up (p95) attracts creative young types – I always meet great people there. **Brown bar** De Engelbewaarder (p130) is a classic – they have boiled eggs on the bar. Interesting conversation is guaranteed. **Hot scene** Bar Italia (p52) gets shoulder-to-shoulder on Fridays. It's a big open space – people eat, then go downstairs to mingle. **Dinner treat** Bo Cinq (p90) – go! It has wonderful modern Moroccan-French food and a cool scene. **Snacks** I love the sticky-toffee cake at Buffet van Odette (p68). **The cocktail scene** Vesper (p77) is really the only other place that has drinks like here.

¶¶ EAT

¶¶ BURGER BAR *Fast Food*   €
☎ 330 59 68; Reguliersbreestraat 9;
🕒 11am-3am Sun-Thu, 11am-4am Fri &
Sat; 🚊 4/9/14 Rembrandtplein; 🚻
Choose your meat, weight and
toppings (grilled onions, goat's
cheese and more), to compose a
fresh, custom burger. Wagyu beef
is an option, as is a portabello
mushroom. Real plates, silverware
and fresh flowers put the experience a cut above fast food.

¶¶ COFFEE & JAZZ *Indonesian* €
☎ 624 58 51; Utrechtsestraat 113;
🕒 11am-11pm Tue-Fri; 🚊 4 Prinsengracht; Ⓥ
'Coffee & Jazz & Surprisingly Tasty
Indonesian Food' isn't quite as
catchy, but more accurate. This
one-man operation is typical eccentric Amsterdam – a must for jazz
freaks and anyone who loves a snug
place with a passionate owner.

¶¶ DE CARROUSEL *Pancakes*   €
☎ 625 80 02; 2e Weteringplantsoen
1; 🕒 10am-9pm; 🚊 4/7/10/16/24/25
Weteringcircuit; 🚻
Join the swarms of kids and
parents from the adjacent playground for big-as-a-dinner-plate
pancakes or smaller *poffertjes*
(minipancakes). True to Dutch
parenting form, adults can get
beers and savoury snacks too.

¶¶ FEBO *Fast Food*   €
☎ 620 86 15; Leidsestraat 94; 🕒 11am-
3am Sun-Thu, 11am-4am Fri & Sat;
🚊 1/2/5 Prinsengracht; 🚻 Ⓥ 🚻
We don't exactly recommend this
Dutch fast-food icon. The *bami*
rolls are hot as napalm, the *frikadel*
frightening and the *kaassoufflé*
utterly unsoufflélike. But plucking
a treat from the yellow automat
windows is a drunken Dutch
tradition. And the *frites* (from
the counter) are pretty good,
complete with sauce on the side.
There's another near Rembrandtplein (Reguliersbreestraat 38), but
for deep-fried goodness in that
area, don't miss Van Dobben (p90).

¶¶ LOS PILONES *Mexican*   €€
☎ 320 46 51; Kerkstraat 63; 🕒 4-
11.30pm Tue-Sun; 🚊 1/2/5 Prinsengracht; Ⓥ 🚻
Yes, this place has excellent
Mexican food, cooked by Mexi-
cans who know what dishes like
cochinita pibil should taste like. But
that's probably not why you came
to Amsterdam; we recommend it
more because it's a quality place
that, with its colourful, casual
fiesta atmosphere, is also child-
friendly.

¶¶ MAOZ *Fast Food*   €
☎ 420 74 35; Muntplein 1; 🕒 11am-
1am Sun-Thu, 11am-3pm Fri & Sat;
🚊 4/9/14/24/25 Muntplein; 🚻 Ⓥ 🚻

HOW TO EAT A HERRING

'Hollandse Nieuwe' isn't a fashion trend – it's the fresh catch of supertasty herring, raked in every June. The season's precise start date depends on when the little fish reach their prime fattiness, and it's greeted with all the fanfare that the new Beaujolais would be elsewhere. Although Dutch tradition calls for dangling the *haring* above your mouth, this isn't the way it's done in Amsterdam. Here the fish is served chopped in chunks, and eaten with a tooth-pick, topped with *eitjes* (chopped onions) and *zuur* (sweet pickles). A *broodje haring* is even handier, as the fluffy white roll holds on the toppings and keeps your fingers fish-fat-free – think of it as an edible napkin.

Falafel, saviour of vegetarians the world over, is perfected at this mini-chain, which has now expanded beyond the Netherlands. Just €4 gets you a falafel with unlimited access to a massive salad bar – a true test of your pita's strength. There's another outlet at Leidsestraat 85.

PATA NEGRA *Spanish* €€
☎ 422 62 50; Utrechtsestraat 124;
noon-midnight Sun-Thu, noon-1am Fri & Sat; 4 Prinsengracht
Pata Negra has been around since 1997, dishing up supergarlicky prawns, grilled sardines and other savoury treats. It can get impossibly crowded, especially on weekends – arrive before 6.30pm or reserve a table. The kitchen is open until 11pm (11.30pm on weekends).

TASTE OF CULTURE
Chinese €
☎ 427 11 36; Korte Leidsedwarsstraat 139-141; 5pm-1am Sun-Thu, 5pm-3am Fri & Sat; 1/2/5/7/10 Leidseplein;

Most restaurants near the Leidseplein dish up greasy stuff for tourists and late-night drinkers, but this one bucks the trend, with freshly prepared regional dishes, enjoyed by a big Chinese clientele. Good options are the razor clams and various stir-fried greens. Added bonus: the kitchen is open till midnight, and later on weekends.

TEMPO DOELOE
Indonesian €€
☎ 625 67 18; Utrechtsestraat 75; 6-11.30pm; 4 Keizersgracht; V
This is one of Amsterdam's most respected Indonesian restaurants. It's a slightly formal place that gives solo diners a chance to try the sampler-plate *rijsttafel* (many places will do it only for a minimum of two people). But the à la carte options are arguably better. Reservations are required – or visit the owners' more casual Tujuh Maret next door.

☷ VAN DOBBEN
Sandwich Shop   €

☎ 624 42 00; Korte Reguliersdwars-straat 5; ⏱ 9.30am-1am Mon-Fri, 9.30am-2am Sat, 11.30am-8pm Sun; 🚇 4/9/14 Rembrandtplein

Open since the 1940s, the venerable Van Dobben has white tile walls, white-coated counter men who brusquely take your order, white glasses of milk next to fluffy white *broodje* rolls. The only colour comes from the meat – heaps of sliced roast beef glow like rubies, and your much-Dutcher-than-you neighbour is probably eating a glistening red plate of steak tartare. Try the *pekelvlees* (something resembling corned beef), or make it a *halfom,* if you're keen on that being mixed with liver.

☷ WALEM *Cafe*   €

☎ 625 35 44; Keizersgracht 449; ⏱ 9am-1am Sun-Thu, 9am-2am Fri & Sat; 🚇 1/2/5 Keizersgracht

Two terraces, friendly service and a changing menu keep this grand cafe, which is run by the same team who do a solid job at De Jaren (p47), popular. There's a line of soups and salads, as well as a few simple mains, but overall it's just a great place to chill out, regroup and appreciate the industrial-mod style of this great Gerrit Rietveld building.

☷ WOK TO WALK *Chinese*   €

☎ 624 29 41; Leidsestraat 96; ⏱ 11.30am-1am Sun-Thu, 11.30am-3am Fri & Sat; 🚇 1/2/5 Prinsengracht; ♿ 🅥

Many fast-food joints in Amsterdam assume you're too drunk or stoned to care what you're eating. Wok to Walk, however, serves fast food fresh. Choose noodles or rice, meat or veg, and a sauce; add to a wok and stir. There are other branches around town, wherever drunk people gather.

☒ DRINK

☒ BARNEY'S LOUNGE
Coffeeshop

☎ 420 66 55; Reguliersgracht 27; ⏱ 9am-1am; 🚇 4 Keizersgracht

A branch of the Haarlemmerdijk institution (p73), located on a beautiful and quiet stretch of canal.

☒ BO CINQ *Lounge*

☎ 622 06 82; Prinsengracht 494; ⏱ noon-1am Sun-Thu, noon-2am Fri & Sat; 🚇 1/2/5 Prinsengracht

Mid-East chic is the look at this moodily lit modern lounge, favoured by flashier Amsterdammers. Snack on spicy lamb minipizzas and sip a drink by the long, sleek bar. There's a full restaurant as well, but it's more style than substance.

☷ CAFÉ AMERICAIN *Cafe*
☎ 556 32 32; Leidsekade 97; ☽ 7am-10pm; ☷ 1/2/5/7/10 Leidseplein
The art deco interior of this grand cafe, with its vaulted ceiling and stained-glass windows, is one of Amsterdam's most stylish and easily justifies a drink or two here, if only to have a peek.

☷ CAFÉ SCHILLER *Cafe*
☎ 624 98 46; Rembrandtplein 24a; ☷ 4/9/14 Rembrandtplein
With a fabulous art deco interior, this is the sole piece of old-fashioned charm on the raucous Rembrandtplein. Walls are lined with portraits of long-dead Dutch actors and cabaret artists, and tippling journalists often occupy the bar stools and booths.

☷ DE HUYSCHKAEMER *Bar*
☎ 627 05 75; Utrechtsestraat 137; ☷ 4 Prinsengracht
Of all the bars along Utrechtsestraat, this one attracts the most mixed crowd – gay and straight, expat and local, old and young – and it spills out onto the sidewalk on weekends. The setting is an old-fashioned split-level room, but the decor is modern, with sleek booths along the walls.

☷ DE KOFFIE SALON *Cafe*
☎ 330 43 12; Utrechtsestraat 130; ☽ 7am-7pm; ☷ 4 Prinsengracht; Ⓥ ☷

Stay in and sip your coffee in this split-level lounge (there's a couch section upstairs) or take it to go, a relative rarity in this city. The baristas are cheerful and friendly, and there are *stroopwafels* (thin waffles filled with syrup) and other goodies from Lanskroon (p50).

☷ DOOR 74 *Bar*
☎ 063 404 51 22; Reguliersdwarsstraat 74; ☽ 8pm-3am Tue-Thu & Sun, 8pm-4am Fri & Sat; ☷ 9/14 Rembrandtplein
Far and away Amsterdam's best cocktails, served in an elegant but unpretentious atmosphere, behind an unmarked door. Send a text message to reserve a seat.

☷ ROKERIJ *Coffeeshop*
☎ 422 66 43; Lange Leidsedwarsstraat 41; ☽ 10am-1am; ☷ 1/2/5 Prinsengracht
Behind the black hole of an entrance you'll find Asian decor and candlelight for those tired of the Rastafarian vibe. There's another, tiny branch at Amstel 8.

☷ VIVELAVIE *Gay & Lesbian*
☎ 624 01 14; Amstelstraat 7; ☽ 4pm-3am Sun-Thu, 4pm-4am Fri & Sat; ☷ 4/9/14 Rembrandtplein
Amsterdam's most popular lesbian bar has friendly bar staff, great music, and a lovely summer terrace. It's a great place for a late-night drink.

▼ WEBER *Lounge*

☎ 622 99 10; Marnixstraat 397;
☽ 8pm-3am Mon-Thu, 8pm-4am Fri-Sun; 🚃 1/2/5/7/10 Leidseplein

A great buzzy bar with loud indie music and a less pretentious vibe than the overtly hip decor might suggest. The only catch is that it's impossibly small, but the owners solved that by opening neighbouring Kamer 401 (at Marnixstraat 401) and Lux (next door at Marnixstraat 403); the latter is practically a mirror image of Weber – confusing after a couple of drinks.

★ PLAY

☆ AIR *Nightclub*

☎ 820 06 70; www.air.nl; Amstelstraat 16; admission €15; ☽ Thu-Sun; 🚃 4/9/14 Rembrandtplein

This club opening was the biggest nightlife event of 2010, as it revives a legendary club space that had long been empty. It's the venue DJs now hanker to play. Some 1300 dancers can pack in, but side rooms make it cosier. Thursday night's 3Hoog party has cheaper entry.

For the best English-language comedy in town, check out a Boom Chicago show

⭐ BOOM CHICAGO *Comedy*

☎ 423 01 01; www.boomchicago.nl; Leidseplein 12; admisslon €13-24; ⏱ box office 11.30am-8.30pm; 🚊 1/2/5/7/10 Leidseplein; ♿

This hilarious English-language improv troupe has been playing to enthusiastic crowds since 1993, and its members have gone on to *Saturday Night Live*, *The Colbert Report* and other American comedy mainstays. The topical shows riff on local and European issues – it's a surprisingly good place to get the pulse of Amsterdam politics.

⭐ ESCAPE *Nightclub*

☎ 622 11 11; www.escape.nl, in Dutch; Rembrandtplein 11; ⏱ 11pm-4am Thu, 11pm-5am Fri & Sat, 11pm-4.30am Sun; 🚊 4/9/14 Rembrandtplein; ♿

Amsterdam's biggest, glitziest club has managed to keep the bass pumping since the '80s; it got a major tech revamp in 2007. Except for the once-a-month gay night, the scene can be pretty generic, with a long line at the door to boot – we recommend it only if there's a well-known DJ at the helm.

⭐ JAZZ CAFÉ ALTO *Live Music*

☎ 626 32 49; www.jazz-cafe-alto.nl; Korte Leidsedwarsstraat 115; admission free; ⏱ 9pm-3am Sun-Thu, 9pm-4am Fri & Sat; 🚊 1/2/5/7/10 Leidseplein

Smack in Amsterdam's touristy heart is this renowned gem of a jazz club – it's so small that you feel as though you're part of the musical conversation between the band members. Admittedly, drinks are a little pricey (to make up for the free admission), but not outrageous.

⭐ JIMMY WOO *Nightclub*

☎ 626 31 50; www.jimmywoo.com; Korte Leidsedwarsstraat 18; ⏱ 11pm-3am Thu & Sun, 11pm-4am Fri & Sat; 🚊 1/2/5/7/10 Leidseplein

Opium-den decor and a very serious door policy keep the intimate domain of Jimmy Woo at the top of the cool list, at least among Amsterdam's rich and beautiful. If you're up for it, dress glam, be sweet to the door staff and get on a list if you can, perhaps through your hotel.

GET *UIT* AND ABOUT

Not sure how to spend your evening? Head to the last-minute ticket desk at the **Uitburo** (☎ 621 13 11; www .aub.nl; ⏱ 10am-7.30pm Mon-Sat, noon-6pm Sun), in the corner of the Stadsschouwburg on the Leidseplein. Comedy, dance, concerts, even club nights are all potentially available at a significant discount – and handily marked 'LNP' (language no problem) if the event doesn't hinge on understanding Dutch to have fun.

Universal appeal: the Melkweg arts centre has something for everyone

⭐ MELKWEG *Arts Centre*
☎ 531 81 81; www.melkweg.nl;
Lijnbaansgracht 234a; 🚊 1/2/5/7/10
Leidseplein; ♿

The Milky Way – it's housed in a former dairy – must be the city's coolest club-gallery-cinema-cafe-concert hall. Its vibrant program of events is so full and varied that it's impossible not to find something you want to go to, from international DJ club nights to live Brazilian jazz.

⭐ PARADISO
Nightclub, Live Music
☎ 626 54 61; www.paradiso.nl; Wetering-schans 6-8; 🚊 7/10 Spiegelgracht;
Amsterdam's best live-music venue, set in a former church, attracts big names despite its relatively small

size. After the bands finish Friday through Sunday, the space becomes an excellent, no-pretensions club with interesting dance music, anything from Finnish DJs spinning jazz to Afro New Wave from New York and tech-hop from Detroit. Admission varies according to the night, from free to €25.

⭐ STADSSCHOUWBURG
Concert Hall, Theatre
☎ 624 23 11; www.ssba.nl, in Dutch;
Leidseplein 26; tickets €12-80; ⏰ box office 10am-6pm; 🚊 1/2/5/7/10
Leidseplein; ♿

This beautiful baroque building is the city's most impressive theatre, hosting large-scale touring productions, dance and drama by Toneelgroep Amsterdam.

⭐ STUDIO 80 *Nightclub*

☎ 521 83 33; www.studio-80.nl, in Dutch; Rembrandtplein 17; ⏰ Wed-Sat; 🚊 4/9/14 Rembrandtplein

It's all about the (electronic) music at this raw space, which functions as much as a studio and radio station as a club. It hosts parties several nights a week – the M.U.L.T.I.S.E.X.I. bash is one of the most popular. Cheap entry guarantees a young crowd.

⭐ SUGAR FACTORY

Live Music, Nightclub

☎ 626 50 06; www.sugarfactory.nl; Lijnbaansgracht 238; ⏰ 6.30pm-1am Mon-Thu, 6.30pm-2am Fri & Sat, 7pm-1am Sun; 🚊 1/2/5/7/10 Leidseplein

One night it's Balkan beats; another, it's a 10-piece soul ensemble. The Sugar Factory has all kinds of live entertainment, usually with a band around 8pm, followed by a dance club night on weekends. Equally important, the vibe is always welcoming and creative. It's an excellent midsize space, with a smoking lounge upstairs.

⭐ TWSTD *Live Music*

☎ 320 70 30; Weteringschans 157; ⏰ 6pm-1am Sun-Thu, 6pm-4am Fri & Sat; 🚊 16/24/25 Weteringcircuit

This tiny bar supports an outsize DJ scene, with unknowns as well as celebs working the wheels of steel every night of the week. There's barely room to wiggle your hips, but it's a good place to chill out, and ask about bigger dance parties.

⭐ UP *Nightclub*

☎ 623 69 85; www.clubup.nl; Korte Leidsedwarsstraat 26; admission €6-10; ⏰ Thu-Sun; 🚊 1/2/5/7/10 Leidseplein

Private arts society De Kring sponsors this small, quirky club, where you could encounter DJs, live bands, performance art – all for a young, eclectic crowd. Occasionally entrance is through De Kring, at Kleine Gartmanplantsoen 7-9; check the website.

>VONDELPARK & OLD SOUTH

Canny Amsterdammers financed Vondelpark in the 1860s by reclaiming more land than necessary, then selling the excess to developers on the condition that no factories or workers' cottages be built. Thus arose Oud Zuid (Old South), one of Amsterdam's most gracious neighbourhoods, and one of its wealthiest. The tree-shaded old homes along the park are a beautiful area to wander aimlessly – the houses get bigger the further south you go.

Adjacent to all this are the city's best art collections. The Rijksmuseum (p98) is the granddaddy, an 1885 Dutch Renaissance–style behemoth by PJH Cuypers, who also designed Centraal Station. When it and the nearby Concertgebouw (1888) were built, the area between them was still farmland. Now it's a big patch of grass called Museumplein, handy for footsore tourists and well used by locals too, especially in winter, when an ice-skating rink is installed. There's a cafe on the north side (check out the toilets!), a skate ramp and the highly photogenic 'I amsterdam' sign.

VONDELPARK & OLD SOUTH

🔵 SEE
Openluchttheater	1	C2
Rijksmuseum	2	F2
Rijksmuseum Entrance (temporary)	3	F2
Stedelijk Museum	4	E2
Van Gogh Museum	5	E2
Vondelpark Main Entrance	6	E1

🟠 SHOP
& Klevering	7	D3
Coster Diamonds	8	E2
Fred de la Bretonière	9	E2
Marlies Dekkers	10	C3

Pauw	11	E2
Pied à Terre	12	D1
Van Avezaath Beune	13	D3

🍴 EAT
Albert Heijn	14	E2
Brasserie Bark	15	E3
De Peper	(see 29)	
Het Groot Melkhuis	16	C2
La Falote	17	F4
Loetje	18	F3
Overtoom Groente en Fruit	19	D1
't Blauwe Theehuis	20	D2
Vertigo	(see 27)	

🍸 DRINK
De Koffie Salon	21	D1
Hollandsche Manege	22	D1
Welling	23	D3
Wildschut	24	E3

⭐ PLAY
Concertgebouw	25	E3
De Vondeltuin	26	A3
Eye	27	D1
Orgelpark	28	B2
OT301	29	C2
SMART Project Space	30	C1

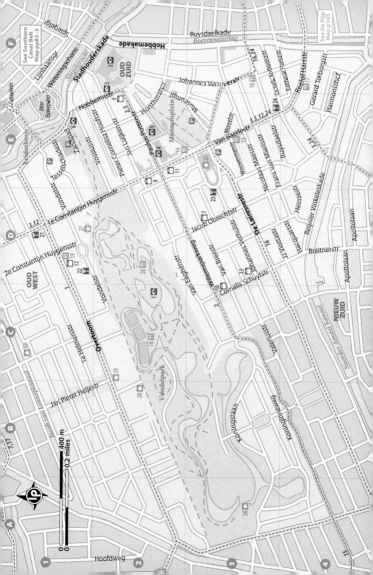

◉ SEE

◉ RIJKSMUSEUM

☎ 674 70 00; www.rijksmuseum.nl; Jan Luijkenstraat 1; adult/child under 18yr €12.50/free; ⏱ 9am-6pm; 🚊 2/5 Hobbemastraat; ♿

The city's main art attraction can get mobbed, so it helps to buy tickets online and bypass the queue. A leisurely stroll through the 'greatest hits' collection takes about two hours. Also poke around in the museum's gardens (free), which are dotted with sculpture and pieces of architectural detail.

◉ STEDELIJK MUSEUM

www.stedelijk.nl; Paulus Potterstraat 13; 🚊 2/3/5/12 Van Baerlestraat
Amsterdam's cutting-edge contemporary art collection is closed until late 2011 for renovations, which include adding an entrance that locals have dubbed 'the Bathtub'.

◉ VAN GOGH MUSEUM

☎ 570 52 00; www.vangoghmuseum.nl; Paulus Potterstraat 7; adult/child under 17yr €14/free; ⏱ 10am-6pm Sat-Thu, 10am-10pm Fri; 🚊 2/3/5/12 Van Baerlestraat; ♿

Spend some quality time with Vincent at the impressive Van Gogh Museum

FRIDAY NIGHT SKATE

This weekly event (www.fridaynightskate.com) is a great way to see the city. You'll also get to meet new people: hundreds of in-line skaters (perhaps thousands in peak season) gather at 8pm near the Eye in Vondelpark for departure at 8.30pm. The route varies each week, but generally it's a challenging 15km or 20km – you should be an experienced skater to participate. The event is cancelled if streets are wet, meaning that on average it actually takes place about twice a month. Rent skates at **De Vondeltuin** (☎ 062 756 55 76; www .vondeltuin.nl, in Dutch; Vondelpark 7; skate rental per 1hr/2hr/3hr adult €5/7.50/10; ⏱ Mar-Oct), at the south end of the park.

The artist's sunflowers draw flocks of visitors to the Van Gogh Museum, so as with the other major museums throughout town, it's possible to purchase tickets online and avoid the lengthy queues. Perhaps even more appealing is a visit on a Friday evening, when it hosts some kind of live music and there's a party atmosphere. Until the Stedelijk Museum (opposite) reopens, the back wing here will mount a few temporary shows of its neighbour's art collection.

🄲 VONDELPARK
Stadhouderskade; ⏱ 24hr; 🚊 2/5 Hobbemastraat
Enjoying Vondelpark is as simple as picking out your patch of grass. But for a proper chair, head to **Vertigo** (☎ 612 30 21; ⏱ 11am-1am Mon-Fri, 10am-1am Sat & Sun), the cafe at the Eye (p103), or **'t Blauwe Theehuis** (☎ 662 02 54; ⏱ 9am-10pm), a cafe in a mod building that looks like a flying saucer. It

has 700 or so terrace seats for sun-lovers. Parents can let their kids roam at **Het Groot Melkhuis** (☎ 612 96 74; ⏱ 10am-dusk; 🄳), a self-service cafe adjacent to a huge playground. For entertainment, catch an organ concert at **Orgelpark** (☎ 515 81 11; www.orgelpark .nl, in Dutch; Gerard Brandtstraat 26; tickets €12.50/7.50) or check the schedule at the **Openluchttheater** (☎ 428 33 60; www.openluchttheater.nl), an outdoor stage with drama, live jazz, kids' shows and more – all with free admission.

SHOP

🄲 & KLEVERING *Housewares*
☎ 670 36 23; Jacob Obrechtstraat 19a; 🚊 2 Jacob Obrechtstraat
If it's quirky, colourful and sits on your table, it's sure to be in this fun home-accessories shop. This is the place to pick up a great example of Dutch-designed cleverness without blowing your budget.

🔲 COSTER DIAMONDS
Jewellery
☎ 305 55 55; Paulus Potterstraat 2-6;
🕙 9am-5pm; 🚋 2/5 Hobbemastraat
Founded in 1840, Coster is a
trustworthy retail shop. Watch the
polishers at work – more interesting than the overrated **Diamant
Museum** (admission €7.50/5) you're led
into at the end.

🔲 FRED DE LA BRETONIÈRE
Footwear
☎ 470 93 20; Van Baerlestraat 34;
🕙 1-6pm Mon, 10am-6pm Tue, Wed &
Fri, 10am-9pm Thu, 10am-5pm Sat, 1-
5pm Sun; 🚋 2/3/5/12 Van Baerlestraat
A branch of the sensible-yet-fun
Dutch shoe shop (p45).

🔲 MARLIES DEKKERS *Clothing*
☎ 471 41 46; Cornelis Schuytstraat 13;
🕙 Mon-Sat; 🚋 2 Cornelis Schuytstraat
With a fireplace and chandeliers,
and bonbons to nibble, this shop
is the perfect setting for the gorgeous, racy work of Dutch lingerie
designer Dekkers (her 'bare butt
dress' is ensconced in a Rotterdam
design museum).

🔲 PAUW *Clothing*
☎ 671 73 22; Van Baerlestraat 72;
🚋 2/3/5/12 Van Baerlestraat
Pauw means 'peacock', but the
clothes at this elegant Dutch
minichain are more formal than
flashy, with taffeta in gemlike

shades, equestrian-style coats and
sculptural blouses. There's a men's
shop down the road at No 90, and
another women's shop at No 66.

🔲 PIED À TERRE *Books*
☎ 627 44 55; Overtoom 135-137;
🕙 Mon-Sat; 🚋 1 1e Constantijn
Huygensstraat
With galleries and a skylight, this
travel-book shop feels like a Renaissance centre of learning. It stocks
hiking and cycling tomes, topo-
graphical maps and assorted travel
guides, including many in English.

🔲 VAN AVEZAATH BEUNE
Food & Drink
☎ 624 83 56; Johannes Verhulststraat 98;
🕙 Tue-Sat; 🚋 2 Cornelis Schuytstraat
This century-old sweets specialist
is known for its boxes of chocolates in the shape of *amster-
dammertjes,* the bollards along city
sidewalks – a great gift, if you can
keep yourself from eating them.

🍴 EAT
🍴 ALBERT HEIJN
Supermarket   €
☎ 662 04 16; Van Baerlestraat 33a;
🕙 8am-10pm; 🚋 3/5/12/16/24 Museumplein; Ⓥ ♿ 👶
The big supermarket chain has
a prime branch hidden beneath
Museumplein – great for picnic
provisions.

☎ BRASSERIE BARK
Seafood €€

☎ 675 02 10; Van Baerlestraat 120;
⏲ lunch Mon-Fri, dinner till 12.30am
daily; 🚊 3/5/12/16/24 Museumplein
This somewhat old-fashioned spot
gets especially buzzing later in the
evening, due to its generous hours.
It's good for a meal of North Sea
shrimp, lobster and the like after a
show at the Concertgebouw (p102).

☎ DE PEPER *Vegetarian* €

☎ 412 29 54; www.depeper.org;
Overtoom 301; ⏲ 6-8.30pm Tue, Fri &
Sun; 🚊 1 Jan Pieter Heijestraat
The friendly restaurant at the OT301
squat (p103) serves cheap organic
vegan meals – a great place to connect with like-minded folks. Same-
day reservations are required.

☎ LA FALOTE *Dutch* €

☎ 662 54 54; Roelof Hartstraat
26; ⏲ 3-9pm Mon-Fri, 5-9pm Sat;
🚊 3/5/12/24 Roelof Hartplein; 🚻
Echt Nederlands home-style
cooking such as calf's liver or
meatballs with endives. With a daily special coming in at under €10,
this is a bargain in an otherwise
ritzy neighbourhood. Wait till the
owner brings out the accordion.

☎ LOETJE *Dutch* €€

☎ 662 81 73; Johannes Vermeerstraat
52; ⏲ lunch Mon-Fri, dinner Mon-Sat;
🚊 16/24 Ruysdaelstraat; 🚻

This cafe's short menu may be
written on the chalkboard, but
everyone just orders thick steak,
served medium-rare and swim-
ming in delicious brown gravy.
The staff are surprisingly good-
humoured, particularly considering the loud, meat-drunken mobs
they typically serve!

☎ OVERTOOM GROENTE EN
FRUIT *Turkish, Delicatessen* €

☎ 683 98 88; Overtoom 129; ⏲ 9am-
6pm; 🚊 1 1e Constantijn Huygensstraat
This Turkish grocery has a range
of premade salads and snacks,
perfect for picnics in the park.

🍸 DRINK

🍸 DE KOFFIE SALON *Cafe*

☎ 612 40 79; 1e Constantijn
Huygensstraat 82; ⏲ 7am-7pm;
🚊 3/12 Overtoom; 🅥
A branch of the excellent coffee
bar on the Utrechtsestraat (p91).

🍸 HOLLANDSCHE MANEGE
Cafe

☎ 618 09 42; Vondelstraat 140;
⏲ 2-11pm Mon-Thu, 9am-11pm
Wed, 9am-6pm Sat, 9am-5pm Sun;
🚊 1 1e Constantijn Huygensstraat; 🚻
The elegant cafe at this riding
school, built in 1882, is one of
Amsterdam's greatest treasures.
It overlooks the large arena,
softly sunlit and smelling of hay

and horses. To get there, enter through the long arcade on Vondelstraat, take a left turn and head up the stairs.

☑ WELLING *Brown Cafe*
☎ 662 01 55; Jan Willem Brouwersstraat 32; ⏱ 4pm-1am Mon-Fri, 3pm-1am Sat & Sun; 🚊 3/5/12/16/24 Museumplein
Behind the Concertgebouw, this local bar feels more like a library – but one where you're allowed to drink beer and have loud philosophical arguments. Regulars include notable artists and intellectuals, and an excellent cat.

Chill: Vondelpark is just the tonic for sore heads

☑ WILDSCHUT *Cafe*
☎ 676 82 20; Roelof Hartplein 1; 🚊 3/5/12/24 Roelof Hartplein; ♿
In warm weather, join the crowd on the front terrace with a view of Amsterdam School buildings (see boxed text, p106) or, when skies are grey, marvel at the art deco interior. If you're fussy about such things, avoid the orange juice – last we checked it wasn't freshly squeezed.

★ PLAY
✪ CONCERTGEBOUW
Concert Hall
☎ 573 05 11, 671 83 45; www.concertgebouw.nl; Concertgebouwplein 2-6; ⏱ box office 10am-8.15pm; 🚊 3/5/12/24 Museumplein; ♿
Bernard Haitink, celebrated conductor of the Royal Concertgebouw Orchestra, once remarked that this world-famous hall – built in 1888 with near-perfect acoustics – was the orchestra's best instrument. In addition to evening performances, there are free short concerts every Wednesday at 12.30pm from September until the end of June. Those aged 27 or younger can queue for €10 tickets, available 45 minutes before each show.

✪ EYE *Cinema*
Nederlands Filmmuseum; ☎ 589 14 00; www.filmmuseum.nl; Vondelpark

3; admission €7.80; 🚋 1 1e Constantijn Huygensstraat

The museum owns more than 40,000 films and screens everything from silent classics to contemporary Iranian art house in its Vondelpark pavilion or, during summer, outdoors on the terrace. In late 2011, the Eye will move to a dramatic new building in Amsterdam-Noord – check the website for details.

⭐ OT301 *Arts Centre*

www.squat.net/overtoom301; Overtoom 301; 🚋 **1 Jan Pieter Heijestraat**
This long-established squat in the former Netherlands Film Academy hosts an eclectic roster of bands and DJs, with an emphasis on the strange and fringey.

⭐ SMART PROJECT SPACE
Cinema, Cultural Centre
☎ **427 59 51; www.smartprojectspace .net; Arie Biemondstraat 111;** 🚋 **1 1e Constantijn Huygenstraat**
Once a pathology lab, this big brick complex is now a lab of a different sort, with experimental and art-house film in its two high-tech cinemas, plus avant-garde music in its auditorium. There's also a very good cafe, Lab111; periodically films are screened here too, and the menu reflects the movie.

>DE PIJP

With its narrow streets crowded by a mix of people from all classes and countries, De Pijp is often called the Latin Quarter of Amsterdam. It's come a long way since the 19th century, when it was the city's first move towards unsupervised development. It was also its last, given the dismal results: some of its shoddy tenement blocks collapsed even as they were being built. But the cheap housing harboured artists and intellectuals from early on, and in the 1960s and '70s the government began refurbishing the tenement blocks for immigrants from Morocco, Turkey, Suriname and the Netherlands Antilles.

Since the 1990s, the area has become very desirable for young couples, as well as a sizeable gay population. The numerous cafes, restaurants and bars here have a bohemian feel (even when they're clearly catering to wealthier new Pijp residents). So does lush Sarphatipark, named for a tireless 19th-century philanthropist, Samuel Sarphati, who fought to improve health and housing conditions here. How pleased he'd be to see the place now!

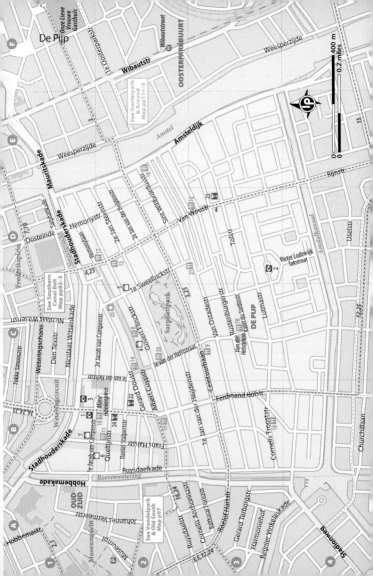

De Pijp

OUD ZUID

OOSTERPARKBUURT

DE PIJP

See Oosterpark
& Around
Map pp114–5

See Southern
Canal Belt
Map pp82–3

See Vondelpark
& South
Map p97

Onze Lieve
Vrouwe
Gasthuis

Wibautstraat

Wibautstr

Weesperzijde

1e Oosterparkstr

Weesperzijde

Amstel

Amsteldijk

Rijnstr

Mauritskade

Sarphatikade

Stadhouderskade

Hemonystr

Hemonylaan

2e Jan Steenstr

1e Jan van der Heijdenstr

Sint Willibrordusstr

Van Woustr

Amstelkanaal

IJselstr

Oosteinde

Frederiksplein

Nicolaas Witsenstr

Weteringschans

Den Texstr

Fokke Simonszstr

Pieter Lodewijk
Takstraat

Tolstr

Lutmastr

Van Ostadestr

Rustenburgerstr

Van der
Helstplein

Kafé du Jardin

Churchilllaan

Sarphatipark

1e Jacob van Campenstr

2e Jacob van Campenstr

Gerard Doustr

Albert Cuypstr

Govert Flinckstr

1e van der Helststraat

1e van der Helststraat

Te Sweelinckstr

Centuurbaan

1e Jan van der Heijdenstr

Ferdinand Bolstr

Cornelis Troststr

Weteringcircuit

Marie
Heinekenplein

Quellijnstr

Daniel Stalpertstr

Frans Halsstr

1e Jacob van Campenstr

Ruysdaelkade

Boerenwetering

Ruysdaelstr

Cornelis Anthoniszstr

Balthasar Floriszstr

Roelof Hartstr

Gerard Terborgstr

Harmoniehof

Reijnier Vinkeleskade

Stadionweg

Hobbemakade

Hobbemastr

Museumplein

Johannes Vermeerstr

Stadhouderskade

N 400 m
0.2 miles

SEE

DE APPEL

☎ 622 56 51; www.deappel.nl; 1e Jacob van Campenstraat 59; admission €7; 🕙 11am-6pm Tue-Sun; 🚊 16/24 Stadhouderskade

This contemporary art space, established in 1975 to show performance art, puts conceptual work in the context of everyday life. The curators have a knack for tapping young international talent, and shows often involve performance or installations around the city.

DE DAGERAAD

Lutmastraat; 🚊 12/25 Cornelis Troostplein; ♿

One of the best Amsterdam School housing projects aside from Het Schip (boxed text, p78), 'The Dawn' is worth a visit if you're an architecture buff. The central structure, on PL Takstraat, is a dramatic curving staircase.

HEINEKEN EXPERIENCE

☎ 523 92 22; www.heinekenexperience.com; Stadhouderskade 78; admission €15; 🕙 11am-7pm, last entry 5.30pm; 🚊 16/24 Stadhouderskade; ♿

Heineken used to be brewed in this very building. Now it's a glitzy multimedia tour, the high price only slightly offset by the three beers you get out of the process. One nice touch, though: you can visit the brewery's sturdy draught horses in their original stables.

SHOP

ALBERT CUYPMARKT
Clothing, Food

Albert Cuypstraat btwn Van Woustraat & Ferdinand Bolstraat; 🕙 10am-5pm Mon-Sat; 🚊 16/24 Albert Cuypstraat

When you're cruising this vast general market, note the shops behind the stalls as well – there's neat fabric, cool clothing and shops like De Peperbol, at No 150,

---

BACK TO SCHOOL

When Amsterdam School architecture started around WWI, it was as much a political movement as an aesthetic one. Architects such as Pieter Kramer and Michel de Klerk were reacting to the decadent, elitist style of neo-Renaissance buildings like Centraal Station, but also to appalling housing conditions for the poor. Their fantastical public-funded housing projects resemble shells, waves and other organic forms; they were obsessive about details, designing everything down to the house numbers. Some details were a bit paternalistic and controlling – windows high in the wall were meant to deter leaning out and gossiping with neighbours – but in general the buildings were vast improvements. Stroll around De Dageraad (above), then visit the museum at Het Schip (p78).

Russell Shorto
Director, John Adams Institute, and author of The Island at the Center of the World

As an American studying Dutch culture, what surprises you? It is a more collectivist society. But when the mayor says, 'We're a city where you can do what you want,' then you can't shop after work because everything's shut – I chafe at that. **Hidden history** I love that the Miracle of Amsterdam (p41) occurred in the house that's now the Amsterdam Dungeon. And De Ysbreeker (p117) is where communists and socialists used to debate. The Nazis entered along the Weesperzijde – I imagine everyone falling silent as they marched past. **Favourite building** The Stopera (p125). It's Amsterdam to mash together civil servants and opera. **Eating out** Stout (p72) is our office clubhouse. But if someone else is paying: Bordewijk (p68). **After midnight** You can get oysters and Champagne at Brasserie Bark (p101). Not that I often do, but it's good to be able to!

which sells bulk spices, kitchen gadgets, essential oils, even Dutch lollies and *zoethout* (liquorice root, good for chewing). Volksrijwielhandel Tornado, at No 214, has high-quality bike accessories. For more on the market, see p19.

 DE EMAILLEKEIZER
Housewares

☎ 664 18 47; 1e Sweelinckstraat 15; ☽ Mon-Sat; ☒ 4/25 Stadhouderskade

Enamel is the stock in trade of this funky shop, which mixes traditional Dutch house numbers, advertising plaques and coffee tins with metal plates and teapots from Poland, Ghana and beyond. You can also nab

African trade beads and Fela Kuti albums.

DE FIETSFABRIEK *Bicycles*

☎ 672 18 34; 1e Jacob van Campenstraat 12; ☽ Tue-Sun; ☒ 16/24 Stadhouderskade

De Fietsfabriek's signature 'box bike' is Amsterdam's equivalent of the double-wide stroller. The creative company has other clever models too, plus fantastic accessories. Custom orders – eg with your name and favourite colour – take four weeks from the factory in Turkey. One of the owners also applies his creativity to cool streetwear, sold at YC Clothing, which is just down the street at No 27.

Leg it to the Albert Cuypmarkt (p106) for some great bargains on food and clothing

🍴 EAT

🍴 BAZAR Turkish €

☎ 675 05 44; Albert Cuypstraat 182;
🕐 11am-midnight Mon-Thu, 11am-2am Fri, 9am-2am Sat, 9am-midnight Sun;
🚊 16/24 Albert Cuypstraat; Ⓥ ⚹

Our four-year-old critic dubbed this hip Mid East cafe 'the most beautiful restaurant in the world'. With plenty of room and tolerant staff, the place is great for young ones, and parents will like the variety of the food. The Turkish breakfast (€8) is particularly nice. Look for the golden angel atop the building.

🍴 COUSCOUS CLUB Moroccan €

☎ 673 35 39; Ceintuurbaan 346;
🕐 dinner Tue-Sun; 🚊 3/25 2e van der Helststraat; Ⓥ

Three types of couscous, three types of cocktails, three desserts – with a straightforward menu, dinner is simple and satisfying at this quirky little restaurant. Gracious staff is a bonus. It's also open after noon for coffee and snacks.

🍴 DE TAART VAN M'N TANTE Bakery & Sweets €

☎ 776 46 00; Ferdinand Bolstraat 10;
🕐 10am-6pm; 🚊 16/24 Stadhouderskade; ♿ Ⓥ ⚹

Entering this bright-pink, Barbie-bedecked cake shop, keep an eye out for children running off their

sugar rush. Once you set eyes on the famous cakes (the designers do wedding creations too), you probably won't notice anything else.

🍴 DE WAAGHALS Vegetarian €€

☎ 679 96 09; Frans Halsstraat 29;
🕐 5-9.30pm Tue-Sun; 🚊 16/24 Stadhouderskade;

The white-walled 'Dare-Devil' is stylish enough that even non-veggies might re-examine their dining priorities. The menu concentrates on one country each month, plus a few staples, such as a rich, mushroom-heavy aubergine daube.

🍴 FIRMA PEKELHAARING Italian €€

☎ 679 0460; Van Woustraat 127-129;
🕐 10am-midnight Mon-Sat; 🚊 4 Lutmastraat; Ⓥ ⚹

Don't let the Dutch name fool you: this is excellent Italian, whether fresh pasta or housemade lamb sausage. Dark wood tables and mismatched modern chairs set a casual-cool tone, and kids get a small stash of toys.

🍴 GAZIANTEP/HARISON'S Turkish €

☎ 618 22 55; Van Woustraat 32; 🕐 8am-5pm; 🚊 4/25 Stadhouderskade; Ⓥ ⚹

The window says Bosnian, but this corner bakery's stock is purely

Turkish, with excellent *lahmacun* (what the Dutch call 'Turkish pizza'), as well as breakfast cookies, savoury pies and big, chewy loaves of bread. Wash it down with some *ayran* (salty yoghurt drink).

🍴 IJSCUYPJE
Bakery & Sweets €

☎ 1e van der Helststraat 27; ⏰ 11am-11pm Mon-Sat, 1pm-11pm Sun; 🚊 16/24 Albert Cuypstraat; ♿ V ☕

Superintense raspberry and rich chocolate make a fantastic combo at this excellent ice-cream stand just off the Albert Cuypmarkt.

🍴 KISMET *Turkish* €

☎ 671 47 68; Albert Cuypstraat 64; ⏰ 10am-10pm; 🚊 16/24 Albert Cuypstraat; V ☕

Primarily a takeout joint, Kismet also has a couple of tables wedged in the back. Either way, it provides good, fresh-tasting Turkish staples such as stuffed eggplant, baked lamb and assorted salads.

🍴 LE HOLLANDAIS
French €€€

☎ 679 12 48; Amsteldijk 41; ⏰ 6.30-10.30pm Mon-Sat; 🚊 3 Amsteldijk

This subdued split-level restaurant doesn't look like much, but it's helmed by a smart, thoughtful chef with a passion for regional

French food. The kitchen makes its own sausages and doesn't shy away from 'variety meats'; sweetbreads and black pudding abound!

🍴 MAOZ
Fast Food €

☎ 676 12 42; Van Woustraat 15; ⏰ 11am-10pm Sun-Thu, 11am-midnight Fri & Sat; 🚊 4/25 Stadhouderskade

A branch of the falafel operation (p88).

🍴 OP DE TUIN
Mediterranean €€

☎ 675 26 20; Karel du Jardinstraat 47; ⏰ 6-10pm Tue-Sun; 🚊 3/25 2e Van der Helststraat; V ☕

This is the kind of informal neighbourhood restaurant where you can sit snacking on an antipasti platter (let the chef decide a mix of Mediterranean standards) or a light pasta dish, and fantasise that you live across the street. Many of the regulars do.

🍴 TJING TJING
South African €€

☎ 676 09 23; Cornelis Troostraat 56-58; ⏰ 2pm-late; 🚊 12/25 Cornelis Troostplein; ♿

You can sample ostrich, springbok and kudu here, but these exotics are secondary to the Cape Malay *bobotie,* a South African shepherd's pie – cooked with passion by the owner. On Sundays during summer, there's an all-you-can-eat *braai* (barbecue).

WARUNG MARLON
Surinamese €

☎ 671 15 26; 1e Van der Helststraat 55; ⏰ 11am-8pm Wed-Mon; 🚊 16/24 Albert Cuypstraat; ♿

Crowds pack the few tables at this informal lunch counter that dishes up cheap, spicy Surinamese-Indonesian food. If you don't want a whole meal, grab a *bakabana* (fried banana) and cup of *dawet* (coconut drink).

WILD MOA PIES
Fast Food €

☎ 064 291 40 50; Van Ostadestraat 147; ⏰ 9am-5.30pm Tue-Sat; 🚊 3/25 2e Van der Helststraat; ♿ V

Inspired by New Zealand, these flaky little handheld meat pies, as well as some tasty vegetarian options, are worth the detour from the Albert Cuypmarkt snack crawl. There's great kiwi hot sauce.

▶ DRINK
▶ GOLLEM *Beer Bar*

☎ 676 71 17; Daniel Stalpertstraat 74; 🚊 16/24 Albert Cuypstraat

A roomier branch of the Belgian beer specialist located in the Centrum (p54).

▶ GREENHOUSE *Coffeeshop*

☎ 673 74 30; Tolstraat 91; ⏰ 9am-1am Sun-Thu, 9am-2am Fri & Sat; 🚊 4 Lutmastraat

The mosaic-trimmed Greenhouse, in an out-of-the-way spot, is spacious and attracts a mostly local crowd. There's a nominal 'membership' process, to keep the rowdies out, but tourists are usually waved through; guys must be 25-plus.

▶ KINGFISHER *Bar*

☎ 671 23 95; Ferdinand Bolstraat 24; ⏰ 11am-1am Mon-Thu, 11am-3am Fri & Sat; 🚊 16/24 Stadhouderskade

Kingfisher's casual brand of cool and laid-back bar staff ensure it's always busy. It's a lot of locals' 'local', and as it's on one of the main streets through De Pijp, it offers great people-watching both inside and out (creative bicyclists are just the start).

PLAY
🟥 DE BADCUYP *Arts Centre*

☎ 675 96 69; www.badcuyp.nl; 1e Sweelinckstraat 10; 🚊 4/25 Stadhouderskade; ♿

A very cool venue off the Albert Cuypmarkt, De Badcuyp reflects the multicultural neighbourhood, with African dance parties, salsa nights and touring artists from all over the world.

>OOSTERPARK & AROUND

The acclaimed Tropenmuseum (opposite), a collection of global ephemera, is a fitting gateway to the quiet neighbourhood Oosterpark, one of the city's most culturally diverse neighbourhoods. Unlike De Pijp (p104), Oosterpark has seen only the tiniest bit of gentrification and it's not (yet) on any trend-watchers' radar – this is precisely what makes it interesting.

A walk east from the museum down Eerste van Swindenstraat leads to the street market on Dapperstraat (opposite) and eventually into Javastraat, where old Dutch fish shops and working-class bars sit adjacent to Moroccan, Indian and Turkish groceries; you'll occasionally spot people 'walking' their birds (in cages), a Surinamese custom. South of Javastraat is considered a so-called 'dish city' – a stretch of apartment blocks studded with satellite dishes which, since the heated immigration debates of 2002, have become the symbols of what many Dutch consider to be 'unassimilated' foreigners.

After a cheap and tasty lunch the best place to relax is the district's namesake, Oosterpark, a lush patch of English-style landscaping that dates from the 1880s.

OOSTERPARK & AROUND

Please see over for map

SEE

OOSTERPARK

's-Gravesandestraat; dawn-dusk; 3/7 Beukenweg

Oosterpark was laid out in 1891 to accommodate the nouveau-riche diamond traders who found their fortunes in the South African mines, and it still has an elegant, rambling feel. On the south side, look for two monuments: one commemorates the abolition of slavery in the Netherlands in 1819, and the other, *De Schreeuw* (The Scream), honours free speech and, more specifically, filmmaker Theo van Gogh, who was murdered at the southeast corner of the park in 2004 (p169). On the park's east side, a more subtle monument to Van Gogh is the Spreeksteen, an open-forum 'speakers' corner' set up in 2005. Scheduled talks have given way to more ad-hoc rants, usually in Dutch.

TROPENMUSEUM

568 82 00; www.tropenmuseum.nl; **Linnaeusstraat 2; adult/under 18yr/senior or student €9/free/7.50;** 10am-5pm; 9/10/14 Alexanderplein;

You could spend all day in this utterly absorbing anthropology museum, watching Bollywood clips, peering through windows into faux bazaar stalls and listening to hits on the Mexican jukebox. The museum began as a collection of colonial booty, so the areas covering former Dutch territory are particularly rich, with gorgeous Indonesian jewellery and enormous Polynesian war canoes. The on-site cafe features dishes from around the globe, but you can also head to a neighbourhood restaurant for the real deal.

SHOP

DAPPERMARKT
Street Market

Dapperstraat btwn Mauritskade & Wijttenbachstraat; 9am-5pm Mon-Sat; 3/7 Dapperstraat

Reflecting the Oost's diverse immigrant population, the Dappermarkt is a delight, a heart-warming mix of people, food and multipacks of socks. Though it was crowned the Netherlands' best street market in 2008, on the surface it doesn't seem much different from the Albert Cuypmarkt (p106). To really appreciate it, skip any actual shopping – just stroll and ogle the crowd.

EAT

BEYZADEM Turkish €

665 90 55; **Javastraat 28;** 9am-11pm; 14 Zeeburgerdijk; V

A sweet family-run restaurant, this place has all the usual fast-food items (Turkish pizza, doner kebab), but the real action is in the daily specials, which are deceptively simple yet delicious dishes such as lamb stew with chickpeas.

NEIGHBOURHOODS

OOSTERPARK & AROUND

Head to De Ysbreeker for a touch of class and loads of *gezelligheid*

PATA NEGRA *Spanish* €€
☎ 692 25 06; Reinwardtstraat 1;
🕐 noon-midnight Sun-Thu, noon-1am
Fri & Sat; 🚊 3/7/9 Linnaeusstraat
A branch of the Utrechtsestraat
tapas joint (p89).

ROOPRAM ROTI
Surinamese €
☎ 693 29 02; 1e Van Swindenstraat 4;
🕐 lunch & dinner; 🚊 9 1e Van Swindenstraat; V 🚼
More often than not, there's a line
to the door at this bare-bones and
superdelicious takeout Surinamese place, but don't worry – it
moves speedily. Place your order –
lamb roti 'extra' (with egg), and

a *barra* (lentil doughnut), at the
very least – with the man at the
bar, and don't forget the hot
sauce.

TRINBAGO *Caribbean* €€
☎ 694 58 36; 1e Van Swindenstraat
44; 🕐 dinner Wed-Sun; 🚊 9 1e Van
Swindenstraat; V
West Indian cuisine gets dressed
up – and very nicely too. Spicy
dishes such as callaloo (a tasty
green-leaf vegetable) are cooked
with a grandmother's soulful
touch, but plated up with an artist's eye. 'Calvin's creations' – the
chef-artist-owner's own work –
feature on the menu, and they're
all good.

🍴 VILLA RUYSCH *French* €€

☎ 663 53 66; Ruyschstraat 15;
🕑 10.30am-1am Sun-Thu, 10.30am-2am
Fri & Sat; 🚇 3 Wibautstraat; 🚻 Ⓥ ♿

The Oost is short on stylish eateries, so this grand cafe stands out. Particularly nice is its package breakfast: eggs baked with cheese, a perfectly flaky croissant and homemade preserves. At night, it's on to cocktails and a menu of French bistro fare. There's lots of outdoor seating, but then you'd miss out on the gorgeous interior, which glitters with Murano-glass mosaics and other flash details.

🍴 VISHANDEL RINKOEN *Seafood* €

☎ 463 11 18; Sumatrastraat 98;
🕑 9am-4.30pm Mon-Sat; 🚇 3/7
Muiderpoortstation

Like other Moroccan-run fish shops in this neighbourhood, this one doubles as a restaurant – pick out what you like from the case and it's cooked up and served at the tables in the next room. Whole prawns arrive in garlicky sauce, calamari is delectably fried and the fish soup is rich – and it all comes in at about €10 per person.

🍸 DRINK

🍸 DE YSBREEKER *Brown Cafe*

☎ 468 18 08; Weesperzijde 23; 🕑 8am-
1am Sun-Thu, 8am-2am Fri & Sat; 🚇 3
Wibautstraat; Ⓥ ♿

Pull up a chair on the terrace at this lovely cafe on the Amstel and it's hard to decide whether to face the beautiful buildings or the gleaming river lined with houseboats. Inside used to house a major jazz and avant-garde music club – that institution has become the Muziekgebouw aan 't IJ (p139), leaving more room here for drinkers in the plush booths and along the marble bar.

WORTH THE TRIP

While everyone's packed into Vondelpark, you'll have room to roam in rustic **Frankendael Park** – and have great food while you're there. One of the city's top restaurants, the lovely **De Kas** (☎ 462 45 62; www.restaurantdekas.nl; Kamerlingh Onneslaan 3; 🕑 noon-2pm Mon-Fri, 6.30-10pm Mon-Sat; ♿ Ⓥ), set in a glittering 19th-century greenhouse, grows its own produce and picks it fresh each morning to compose the single set menu – five courses at dinner (€49.50), four at lunch (€37.50). Vegetarians are treated very well. For a snack, **Merkelbach** (☎ 645 08 80; Middenweg 72; 🕑 8.30am-11pm) has excellent outdoor seating, overlooking a groomed garden. On the last Sunday of each month, **De Pure Markt** (🕑 11am-6pm Apr-Jun & Aug-Dec) sets up, with stands from artisanal food and craft producers.

One of the captivating artefacts you'll find housed at the Tropenmuseum (p113)

⭐ PLAY

⭐ CANVAS OP DE 7E *Nightclub*
☎ 716 38 17; www.canvasopde7e.nl, in Dutch; Wibautstraat 150; ⏰ noon-1am, to 3am Fri & Sat; 🚊 3 Wibautstraat; ♿

Take the elevator to the 7th floor for this restaurant-bar-club. Edgy and improvisational, it's the social centre for all the artists with studios in this building, the former *Volkskrant* newspaper office. The sunset view is terrific, heightened by highly creative cocktails for just €5. Check the website for the event schedule and to make sure it's open – these city-approved *broedplaats* (breeding ground) projects often last only a few years.

⭐ DELICATESSEN
Lounge, Arts Centre
☎ 064 181 34 90; www.delicatessenzeeburg.com; Sumatrastraat 32; ⏰ shop noon-5pm Wed-Sat; 🚊 14 Zeeburgerdijk

This odd, improvisational storefront touts 'the taste of art and culture'. By day, it welcomes people to browse tweaked vintage clothing, old records and new paintings and photography. By night, the space hosts bands, films and casual dinners – check the website for the schedule.

⭐ STUDIO K *Arts Centre*
☎ 692 04 22; www.studio-k.nu; Timorplein 62; 🚊 14 Zeeburgerdijk; ♿ 🚹

Sporting two cinemas, space for bands and theatre, an eclectic Greek-Spanish restaurant (open for lunch and dinner from Tuesday to Sunday) and a huge terrace, the student-run Studio K is your one-stop shop for hip culture in the Oost. Stop in for a coffee, and you might wind up staying all night for a dance party...

☆ TO NIGHT *Nightclub*
☎ 850 24 00; www.hotelarena.nl; 's-Gravesandestraat 51; ⏱ Thu-Sat; 🚊 7/10 Korte 's-Gravesendstraat
Hotel Arena's club hosts radically different nights from one evening to the next, from salsa to '90s hits. It's a bit out of the centre, but definitely worth a hike, as your €15-or-less ticket gets you entry into one of the most beautiful spaces in Amsterdam – a marble-trimmed chapel. As an added bonus, the drinks are relatively cheap.

☆ TROPENTHEATER
Concert Hall
☎ 568 85 00; www.tropentheater.nl; Linnaeusstraat 2; 🚊 9/10/14 Alexanderplein; ♿ 🚻
Two halls adjoining the Tropenmuseum welcome performers from Cuba, Lebanon, Kurdistan and beyond. Check the website for the schedule and ticket prices.

☆ TROUW *Nightclub*
☎ 463 77 88; www.trouwamsterdam.nl; Wibautstraat 127; ⏱ restaurant 6.30pm-1am Tue-Sat, club 10.30pm-5am Fri & Sat; 🚊 3 Wibautstraat
Trouw is housed in a former newspaper office. A creative team (known for its legendary parties in a now-defunct post office in the harbour) has made over the printing-press floor into a coolly industrial restaurant with great snack-size plates of international flavours. But it's even more noted for the way-late club nights (and food served till 3am) and cool film program.

NEIGHBOURHOODS

OOSTERPARK & AROUND

>NIEUWMARKT & PLANTAGE

The old centre ends and the more modern city begins at the Nieuwmarkt, a plaza dominated by the ominous-looking Waag, once a city gate, then a weigh house and now one of the many cafes (In de Waag, p128) that make this square a popular afternoon and evening hangout.

To the southeast, Jodenbreestraat leads into the old Jewish quarter. Little remains, in part due to a controversial overhaul in the 1980s, but a few museums and monuments commemorate the community that once flourished here and in the Plantage neighbourhood further east. Laid out as a garden district in the late 17th century, the Plantage was built up only around 1850, and it's still one of the greenest parts of the city. It's bordered to the north by Entrepotdok, a string of nearly 100 19th-century warehouses, also renovated in the 1980s – to much better effect.

A portion of this area is not served by trams; bus and metro details are provided, but the Nieuwmarkt is not a long walk from the Dam or Waterlooplein.

NIEUWMARKT & PLANTAGE

◉ SEE
Artis Zoo 1 E4
Hollandsche
  Schouwburg 2 D4
Hortus Botanicus 3 D4
Joods Historisch
  Museum 4 B4
Portugese-Israelite
  Synagogue 5 C4
Rembrandthuis 6 B3
Scheepvaarthuis 7 C1
Stopera 8 B4
Verzetsmuseum 9 E4
Zuiderkerk 10 A3

◻ SHOP
De Beestenwinkel 11 A4
De Hoed van Tijn ....(see 14)

Droog 12 A4
Het Fort van Sjakoo 13 B4
Joe's Vliegerwinkel 14 A3
't Klompenhuisje 15 A3
Waterlooplein Flea
  Market 16 B4

⅋ EAT
Burgermeester 17 E4
Café Bern 18 B2
Café Kadijk 19 E3
De Tokoman 20 B4
Greetje 21 C2
Hemelse Modder 22 B2
In de Waag 23 B2
Koffiehuis van den
  Volksbond 24 D3
Nam Kee 25 B2
Plancius 26 E4

Soep en Zo 27 B3
Toko Joyce 28 A2

▼ DRINK
Brouwerij 't IJ 29 H4
De Doelen 30 A4
De Engelbewaarder 31 A3
De Sluyswacht 32 B3
Greenhouse 33 B4
Lokaal 't Loosje 34 A2

★ PLAY
Amsterdams Marionetten
  Theater 35 B2
Het Muziektheater 36 B4
TunFun 37 C4

Please see over for map

SEE

ARTIS ZOO
☎ 523 34 81; www.artis.nl; Plantage Kerklaan 38-40; adult/child 3-9yr/senior/child under 3yr €18.50/15/17/free; ⏲ 9am-5pm daily Sep-Mar, 9am-6pm Sun-Fri, 9am-sunset Sat Jun-Aug; 🚊 9/14 Plantage Kerklaan; ♿ 🚼

Founded in 1838, this zoo feels a bit cramped for modern tastes, but the old buildings (some from the earliest days of the Plantage) are beautiful and the grounds are lush. Plus it's heaven for kids, with more than 700 animal species. One genius exhibit: the murky canal cross-section in the aquarium, featuring discarded bikes and creepy eels. If you prefer your nature pinned to a board or stuffed, be sure to stop by the zoo's museum, a trove of taxidermy and other 19th-century relics. You can actually see into part of the zoo from Entrepotdok, just to the north – see if you can spot the oryx and the zebras!

HOLLANDSCHE SCHOUWBURG
☎ 531 03 40; www.hollandscheschouwburg.nl; Plantage Middenlaan 24; admission free; ⏲ 11am-4pm; 🚊 9/14 Plantage Kerklaan

Located in the Jewish quarter, the 1892 Dutch Theatre was renamed the Jewish Theatre by the Nazis in 1941, then used as a deportation centre. Thousands of Jews were sent to death camps from here, and a memorial and exhibition describe this period.

HORTUS BOTANICUS
☎ 625 90 21; www.dehortus.nl; Plantage Middenlaan 2a; admission €7.50/3.50; ⏲ 9am-5pm Feb-Jun & Sep-Nov, 9am-7pm Jul & Aug, 9am-4pm Dec & Jan; 🚊 9/14 Mr Visserplein; ♿

Built in 1682, the Hortus Botanicus began as a breeding ground for exotic species collected by the VOC (Dutch East India Company). Despite its history, the place is rather small and not as lush as you'd expect. There is an interesting collection of South African plants, the world's oldest potted plant (more than 300 years, and looking it), a clever semicircular garden representing the plant kingdom and a pretty cafe. A garden shop sells items like clog-shaped terracotta pots.

JOODS HISTORISCH MUSEUM
Jewish Historical Museum; ☎ 531 03 10; www.jhm.nl; Nieuwe Amstelstraat 1; adult/child 13-17yr/child under 13yr €9/4.50/free, student & senior €6; ⏲ 11am-5pm; 🚊 9/14 Waterlooplein; ♿

The Great Synagogue, dating from 1675, holds exhibits on the Jewish Diaspora in the Netherlands, as

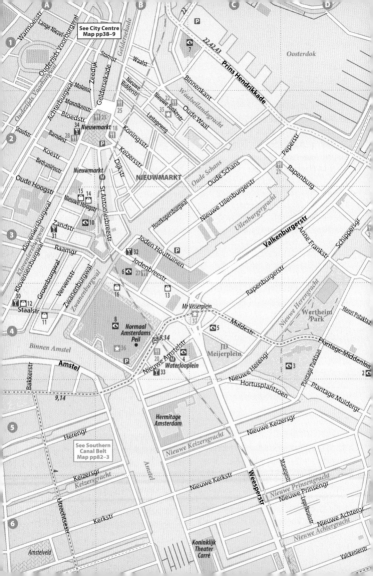

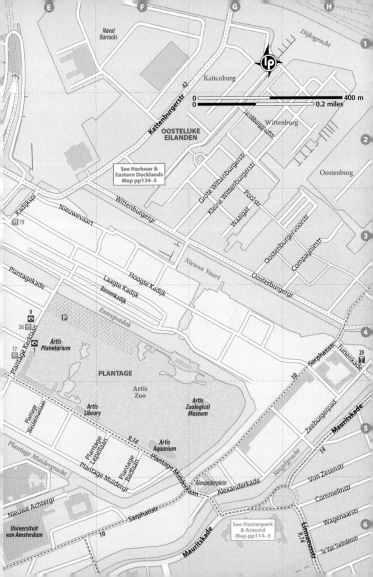

A sample of the flora on show at the Hortus Botanicus (p121)

well as the pillars of Judaism. Perhaps what's most revealing is the room filled with cultural ephemera, which illustrates the Jewish influence in Dutch society – from HEMA stores to the Ajax football team.

PORTUGUESE-ISRAELITE SYNAGOGUE

☎ 624 53 51; www.esnoga.com; Mr Visserplein 3; admission €6.50/4; 🕑 10am-4pm Sun-Fri Apr-Oct, 10am-4pm Sun-Thu, 10am-2pm Fri Nov-Mar; 🚊 9/14 Mr Visserplein

'Hidden' behind a row of single-storey buildings, as per Calvinist policy, this was the largest synagogue in Europe when it was completed in 1675. Its enormous piers were inspired by a model of the Temple of Solomon in Jerusalem (on display at the Bijbels Museum, p62). The interior is austere, with sand on the floorboards and flickering brass chandeliers. If you're visiting the Joods Historisch Museum (p121) as well, get the combo ticket for €12/6.

REMBRANDTHUIS

☎ 520 04 00; www.rembrandthuis.nl; Jodenbreestraat 4; adult/child 7-15yr/ child under 7yr/student €9/2.50/free/6; 🕑 10am-5pm; 🚊 9/14 Waterlooplein; ♿

Rembrandt van Rijn (1606–69) lived and worked in this building for almost 20 years, until poverty forced him into a dumpy flat in the Jordaan. His light filled studio is the highlight, laid out as though he's just nipped down to the kitchen for a bite to eat. Another room is crammed with the art and curiosities that Rembrandt collected – seashells, dried insects, animal horns, busts of Roman emperors and work by other artists. A rotating selection of Rembrandt's etchings is also on display.

SCHEEPVAARTHUIS
Shipping House; Prins Hendrikkade 108; 🚊 **22/32/33/34 Prins Hendrikkade;** ♿
This dark-brick building, built in 1916, was the first true example of Amsterdam School style – and it's still one of the grandest, encrusted in elaborate nautical detailing. Step inside (it's a luxury hotel now) to admire stained glass, gorgeous light fixtures and an amazing staircase.

STOPERA
Waterlooplein; 🚊 **9/14 Waterlooplein**
The city-hall-and-opera-house's portmanteau nickname (stadhuis + opera) also refers to efforts to stop its construction in the 1980s, in hopes of preserving the Jewish district. In the east entrance, visit the **Normaal Amsterdams Peil** (admission free; 🕙 10am-6pm Mon-Sat), the not-quite-sea-level point on which all construction in the country is

calculated. An alarming exhibit shows how much of the city is below the line.

VERZETSMUSEUM
Dutch Resistance Museum; ☎ **620 25 35; www.verzetsmuseum.org; Plantage Kerklaan 61; adult/child 7-15yr/child under 7yr €7.50/4/free;** 🕙 **10am-5pm Tue-Fri, 11am-5pm Sat-Mon;** 🚊 **9/14 Plantage Kerklaan;** ♿
This museum honours the work of the Dutch Resistance and documents gestures large (such as the 1941 dockworkers' strike) and small (document forgery). But it doesn't shy away from the truth that the majority of Dutch Jews were killed during WWII; one chilling display articulates the various reasons many people refused to shelter Jews. Just as interesting is the smaller wing devoted to the Resistance in the Dutch East Indies, which soon after led to independence for Indonesia.

ZUIDERKERK
☎ **622 29 62; Zuiderkerkhof 72;** 🕙 **9am-4pm Mon-Fri, noon-4pm Sat;** Ⓜ **Nieuwmarkt;** ♿
Amsterdam's first Protestant church (1611) was used as a morgue during the 'Hunger Winter' of WWII. Now it's a city-run info centre for Amsterdam's various urban expansion schemes – basically an explanation for all the

construction around town. (Fittingly, next door is the Pentagon, a dreadful 1980s housing complex and mute warning against future bad planning.)

SHOP

DE HOED VAN TIJN
Accessories

☎ 623 27 59; Nieuwe Hoogstraat 15; ◷ noon-6pm Mon, 11am-6pm Tue-Fri, 11am-5.30pm Sat; Ⓜ Nieuwmarkt

An old-fashioned hat shop, with lace-and-flower confections for the ladies and dapper fedoras and more for the gents – as well as a whole range of more practical headwear. The place sells its own designs as well as respected brands.

DE BEESTENWINKEL
Children's

☎ 623 18 05; Staalstraat 26; 🚊 9/14 Waterlooplein

From teeny-tiny teddies to pink plastic pig snouts, this shop is packed to the rafters with *de best* (best) of *de beesten* (animals).

DROOG
Design

☎ 523 50 59; Staalstraat 7b; ◷ 11am-6pm Tue-Sat, noon-5pm Sun; 🚊 4/9/14/16/24/25 Muntplein

Droog means 'dry' in Dutch, and this design house's products are strong on dry wit. The shop is one part playground – there's a big garden swing, and a surprising bench – and one part gallery, which displays limited-edition pieces. But even small items, like superpowerful suction hooks, are seriously smart.

HET FORT VAN SJAKOO
Books

☎ 625 89 79; Jodenbreestraat 24; ◷ 11am-6pm Mon-Fri, 11am-5pm Sat; 🚊 9/14 Waterlooplein

Get the low-down on the squat scene, plus locally produced zines and Trotsky translations, at this lefty bookshop, which has been in operation since 1977.

Sort trash from treasure at Waterloopleinmarkt

FREE MARKET(S)

In addition to the farmers' market and clothes vending on Noordermarkt (p67), Amsterdam has several other interesting street markets that occur periodically. Look out for:

> **Antiques** Nieuwmarkt (Map pp122–3, B2; ☺ 9am-5pm Sun May-Sep); Amstelveld (Map pp82–3, F4; ☺ 9am-6pm last Fri of the month May-Aug)
> **Organic produce** Nieuwmarkt (Map pp122–3, B2; ☺ 9am-3pm Sat); Haarlemmerplein (Map pp60–1, C1; ☺ 9am-2pm Wed)
> **Books** Spui (Map pp38–9, B7; ☺ 8am-6pm Fri)
> **Plants** Amstelveld (Map pp82–3, F4; ☺ 8.30am-1pm Mon Mar-Dec)

🏠 JOE'S VLIEGERWINKEL
Children's
☎ 625 01 39; Nieuwe Hoogstraat 19;
☺ Mon-Sat; Ⓜ Nieuwmarkt
If it flies, it's in stock at this kite specialist. Pick up a colourful starter model for the kids or a deluxe Chinese dragon fighter, and head out to the Museumplein (p96).

🏠 'T KLOMPENHUISJE
Footwear, Children's
☎ 622 81 00; Nieuwe Hoogstraat 9a;
☺ Mon-Sat; Ⓜ Nieuwmarkt
Finely crafted and surprisingly comfortable, traditional Dutch *klompen* (clogs) are just the thing to potter around the garden in. The shop also stocks lots of children's shoes.

🏠 WATERLOOPLEINMARKT
Antiques, Clothing
Waterlooplein; ☺ 9am-5pm Mon-Sat;
🚊 9/14 Waterlooplein; ⓖ
This flea market next to the Stopera (p125) is the place to pick up a funky vintage ensemble, trawl

through piles of €1 clothing, haggle over dented antiques or stock your hippy van with tie-dye bedspreads and a brand-new bong. Don't go too late – by 4.30pm, vendors are more interested in packing up than making a sale.

🍴 EAT

🍴 BURGERMEESTER
International €
☎ 428 02 11; Plantage Kerklaan 37;
☺ noon-11pm; 🚊 9/14 Plantage Kerklaan; Ⓥ ⓖ
At this slick burger joint, don't think American – think organic beef (or lamb, falafel or fish), plus toppings like tarragon mayo and pancetta, to make a fresh, creative sandwich. Sides include roast potatoes and grilled corn on the cob.

🍴 CAFÉ BERN *Swiss* €€
☎ 622 00 34; Nieuwmarkt 9; ☺ dinner;
Ⓜ Nieuwmarkt; Ⓥ ⓖ
People have been flocking to this well-worn brown cafe for

more than 40 years to indulge in gruyère fondue and entrecôte. It's generally closed for a large part of the summer, but do you really want fondue in hot weather anyway?

🍴 CAFÉ KADIJK *Indonesian* €

☎ 061 774 44 11; Kadijksplein 5; ⏱ 4-10pm Mon, noon-10pm Tue-Sun; 🚌 22/42/43/359 Plantage Kerklaan

This hip split-level cafe looks like it can serve no more than coffee from its tiny kitchen, but in fact it does quite good Indonesian food. Go for the *eitjes van Tante Bea*, a spicy mix of egg, shrimp and beans, as well as the rich *rendang* curry. And because it's a cafe, there's *appeltaart* (apple pie) for dessert.

🍴 DE TOKOMAN *Surinamese* €

☎ 421 56 36; Waterlooplein 327; ⏱ 11am-7.30pm Mon-Sat; 🚋 9/14 Waterlooplein; V ♿

We have it on good authority that this has the city's best *broodje pom,* a sandwich filled with a tasty mash of chicken and a starchy Surinamese tuber. You'll want the *zuur* (pickled-cabbage relish) and *peper* (chilli) on it, plus a cold can of coconut water to wash it down. Still hungry? Descend into the Waterlooplein metro stop to rival De Hapjeshoek and nab a *chili kip* or *zoutvlees* sandwich.

🍴 GREETJE
Dutch €€€

☎ 779 74 50; www.restaurantgreetje .nl; Peperstraat 23-25; ⏱ dinner Tue-Sun; M Nieuwmarkt; V

Elegant Greetje will make you reconsider Dutch cuisine. Never mind *stamppot* – here you'll see traditional dishes like leek soup, pickled mackerel and braised oxtail, all composed of market-fresh ingredients and presented beautifully.

🍴 HEMELSE MODDER
Dutch €€

☎ 624 32 03; Oude Waal 11; ⏱ dinner; M Nieuwmarkt; ♿ V

Celery-green walls and blond-wood tables are the backdrop for equally light and unpretentious food, which emphasises North Sea fish and farm-fresh produce. If there's no berry pudding for dessert, the namesake *hemelse modder* (heavenly mud) chocolate mousse is a good fallback.

🍴 IN DE WAAG
International €€

☎ 422 77 72; Nieuwmarkt 4; ⏱ 10am-midnight; M Nieuwmarkt; ♿ V ♿

Prime seats in the centre of the Nieuwmarkt give you a great view of the scene, but don't miss the candlelit interior of this massive historic building. The lunch sandwiches are enormous and there's a good selection of hot dishes beyond that; for dinner though, the prices are unjustifiably high.

KOFFIEHUIS VAN DEN VOLKSBOND
International €€

☎ 622 12 09; Kadijksplein 4; ◷ dinner; 🚌 22/42/43/359 Plantage Kerklaan; Ⓥ 🚼

What began life as a charitable coffee house for dockworkers later got revived by squatters. It still has a fashionably grungy vibe – wood floors, a giant red-rose mural and tall candles on the tables. The ever-changing menu has huge plates of comfort food with ingredients like mussels and Moroccan sausage.

NAM KEE *Chinese* €

☎ 638 28 48; Geldersekade 447; ◷ 4pm-midnight Mon-Fri, 2.30pm-midnight Sat, 2.30-11pm Sun; Ⓜ Nieuwmarkt; Ⓥ

The nicer branch of Amsterdam's Chinese icon (p50).

PLANCIUS
Mediterranean €€

☎ 330 94 69; Plantage Kerklaan 61; ◷ 11am-11pm; 🚌 9/14 Plantage Kerklaan; Ⓥ 🚼

This industrial-chic converted garage offers some nice alternatives to standard sandwiches at lunch: a big messy lamb burger, a great mixed salad, a pasta dish or

two. Dinner dishes tend towards upmarket comfort food. The clientele is mostly TV execs who work nearby.

SOEP EN ZO *Fast Food* €

☎ 422 22 43; Jodenbreestraat 94a; ◷ 11am-8pm Mon-Fri, noon-7pm Sat & Sun; 🚋 9/14 Mr Visserplein; 🚼 Ⓥ

It has uninspiring signage and barely room to move inside, but this soup specialist creates magic in a bowl – or in a takeout container. Daily offerings involve flavours from all over the globe (spicy spinach with coconut, say, or lamb stew). With a warm roll on the side, it's a bargain and a satisfying lunch.

TOKO JOYCE *Indonesian* €

☎ 427 90 91; Nieuwmarkt 38; ◷ 11am-8pm Tue-Sat, 4-8pm Sun & Mon; Ⓜ Nieuwmarkt; Ⓥ 🚼

At this takeaway place, pick and mix a platter of Surinamese-Indonesian food from the glass case – start with spiced yellow rice and add various spicy, coconutty stews. Get a wedge of *spekkoek*, a moist layered gingerbread, to finish.

DRINK
BROUWERIJ 'T IJ *Beer Bar*

☎ 622 83 25; Funenkade 7; ◷ 3-8pm; 🚋 10 Hoogte Kadijk

A de rigueur photo op, plus beer! Amsterdam's leading microbrewery

NEIGHBOURHOODS

NIEUWMARKT & PLANTAGE

NO, YOU'RE NOT DRUNK...

Those buildings *are* leaning. Some (like the Sluyswacht, below) have simply shifted over the centuries, but many canal houses were deliberately constructed to tip forward. Interior staircases were narrow, so owners needed an easy way to move large goods and furniture to the upper floors. The solution: a hoist built into the gable, to lift objects up and in through the windows. The tilt allows loading without bumping into the house front. The forward lean also makes the houses seem larger, which makes it easier to admire the facade and gable – a fortunate coincidence for everyone.

happens to be tucked in the base of De Gooyer windmill, an 18th-century grain mill and the last of five that stood in this area. The house brews are excellent; try the Trappist cheese alongside. Free tours run Friday and Sunday at 4pm.

▼ DE DOELEN *Brown Cafe*
☎ 624 90 23; Kloveniersburgwal 125;
◷ 9am-1am Mon-Thu, 8am-2am Fri & Sat; 🚊 4/9/14/16/24/25 Muntplein
On a busy crossroads between the Amstel and De Wallen (the red-light district), this cafe dates back to 1895 and looks it: carved wooden goat's head, stained-glass lamps, sand on the floor. But there's a fun, youthful atmosphere, and during fine weather the tables spill across the street for picture-perfect canal views.

▼ DE ENGELBEWAARDER
Brown Cafe
☎ 625 37 72; Kloveniersburgwal 59;
🚊 9/14 Waterlooplein

If you like jazz, plan on spending a Sunday afternoon (from 4.30pm) at this small cafe, which has been hosting an open session for decades. The rest of the week, it's a mellow, old-fashioned place to enjoy a beer by the sunny windows.

▼ DE SLUYSWACHT
Brown Cafe
☎ 625 76 11; Jodenbreestraat 1;
🚊 9/14 Waterlooplein
Listing like a ship in a high wind, this tiny black building was once a lock-keeper's house. Today the canalside terrace is one of the nicest spots in town to down a beer, especially after trawling the Waterloopleinmarkt (p127).

▼ GREENHOUSE *Coffeeshop*
☎ 622 54 99; Waterlooplein 345;
◷ 10am-1am Sun-Thu, 9am-2am Fri & Sat; 🚊 9/14 Waterlooplein
A branch of the excellent operation in De Pijp (p111), this place has a 21-plus door policy.

▼ LOKAAL 'T LOOSJE
Brown Cafe

☎ 627 26 35; Nieuwmarkt 32-34;
Ⓜ Nieuwmarkt

With its beautiful etched-glass windows and tile tableaux on the walls, this is one of the oldest and prettiest cafes in the Nieuwmarkt area – a good place to settle in and watch the action on the square.

★ PLAY

✦ AMSTERDAMS MARIONETTEN THEATER *Theatre*

☎ 620 80 27; www.marionettentheater
.nl; Nieuwe Jonkerstraat 8; adult/child under 14yr €15/7.50, student & senior €12; Ⓜ Nieuwmarkt; ♿

This puppet theatre performs Mozart operas such as *The Magic*

If you're so inclined, drop into De Sluyswacht

Flute, enthralling kids (eight years old and up) and adults alike with the fairy-tale stage sets, period costumes and beautiful singing. Shows are roughly twice a month.

✦ HET MUZIEKTHEATER
Concert Hall

☎ 625 54 55; www.hetmuziektheater
.nl; Waterlooplein 22; ✆ box office 10am-6pm Mon-Sat; ⚉ 9/14 Waterloo-plein; ♿

The opera-house half of the Sto-pera (p125), which seats 1600, is home to the Netherlands National Ballet and the Netherlands Opera, known for lavish and creative productions. On Tuesdays from September to May, you can catch free chamber-music concerts in the smaller Boekmanzaal; start time is 12.30pm. For a neat peek behind the scenes, you can take a **tour** (☎ 551 80 54; admission €5) of the building every Saturday at noon.

✦ TUNFUN *Playground*

☎ 689 43 00; www.tunfun.nl; Mr Visser-plein 7; admission free/€7.50; ✆ 10am-6pm; ⚉ 9/14 Mr Visserplein; ♿

An ingenious reuse of a traffic underpass, TunFun is a massive indoor playground, perfect for rainy Amsterdam days. Kids aged one to 12 can build, climb, roll, draw, play indoor soccer and dance, while parents relax in the cafe. Kids must be accompanied by an adult.

>HARBOUR & EASTERN DOCKLANDS

In just a decade, Amsterdam has completely remade its harbour. What used to be the city's fringe – both physically and culturally – has become a centre for culture and sleek modern living. All straight lines and open vistas, the neighbourhood is invigorating to visit if only as a contrast to the city centre, but you'll also want to come out here for a concert at the Muziekgebouw aan 't IJ (p139).

The mighty green NEMO (opposite), erected in 1997, started the new era. Old warehouses and loading docks were gutted and new projects commissioned. Some of the housing blocks can be grim on a grey day, but don't miss the jaunty mismatched blocks on the west end of Java-eiland, the angular silver building dubbed 'the Whale' (at the west end of Sporenburg) and the swooping red footbridges between Borneo-eiland and Sporenburg.

This area is less compact, so it's rewarding and easy to cover by bicycle. There are relatively few bars and cafes, but those that are here make the most of their dramatic location.

HARBOUR & EASTERN DOCKLANDS

🅒 SEE
ARCAM 1 B5
Nederlands
  Scheepvaartmuseum ...2 B5
NEMO 3 B4
Openbare Bibliotheek
  Amsterdam 4 A4

🅐 SHOP
De Ode 5 F3
JC Creations 6 G4
Keet in Huis 7 F3

Pol's Potten 8 F3
Sissy-Boy ....(see 8)

🍴 EAT
De Wereldbol 9 G3
Einde van de Wereld ...10 E3
Fifteen 11 C3
Frank's Smoke House ..12 C5
Gare de l'Est 13 F6
Kompaszaal 14 F3
Roos en Noor 15 G4
Snel 16 F4
Star Ferry 17 B3

🍸 DRINK
Kanis & Meiland 18 F3
KHL 19 F4

⭐ PLAY
Bimhuis 20 B3
Conservatorium van Amster-
  dam 21 A4
Muziekgebouw
  aan 't IJ 22 B3
Panama 23 E4

Please see over for map

◉ SEE

◉ ARCAM

☎ 620 48 78; www.arcam.nl; Prins Hendrikkade 600; ☼ 1-5pm Tue-Sat; 🚊 32/33/34/35/359/361/363 IJ-Tunnel

Located in a stunningly shaped building, Amsterdam's Centre for Architecture (ARCAM) should be the first point of call for architecture and urban design buffs. Staff can suggest buildings to see to match your interests, while the centre also holds regular exhibitions on Dutch and international architecture.

◉ NEDERLANDS SCHEEPVAARTMUSEUM

Netherlands Maritime Museum; ☎ 523 22 22; www.scheepvaartmuseum.nl; Kattenburgerplein 1; 🚊 22/43 Kattenburgerplein

At the time of research the Scheepvaartmuseum was closed for renovation and not scheduled to reopen until the end of 2011. Its full-scale replica of the 700-tonne *Amsterdam* ship is moored by the NEMO (below).

◉ NEMO

☎ 531 32 33; www.e-nemo.nl; Oosterdok 2; adult/under 4yr €12.50/free; ☼ 10am-5pm Tue-Sun Sep-May, daily Jun-Aug; 🚊 32/33/34/35/359/361/363 IJ-Tunnel; ♿

Jutting into the harbour like a ship, Renzo Piano's stunning green-copper edifice is an excellent science and technology museum with hands-on laboratories. On the walk down to the museum, look out for a whole collection of restored cargo ships; you can also visit a beautiful replica of the *Amsterdam* ship (€5, or €15 including NEMO entrance), staffed with grubby-looking pirates who sing sea shanties and conduct burials at sea every hour. NEMO's stepped roof (admission free) is the city's largest summer terrace.

With a building like this, it's not hard to find NEMO

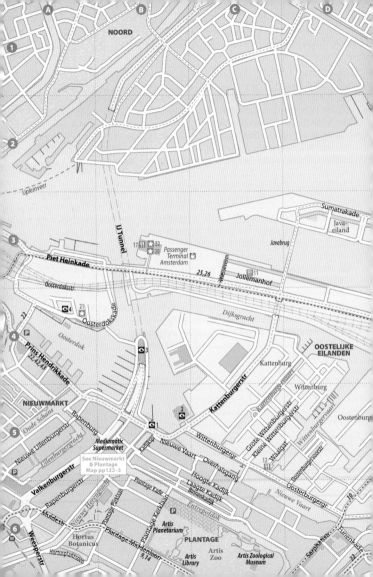

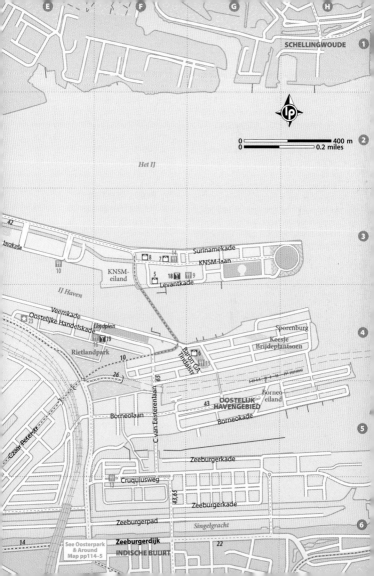

NEIGHBOURHOODS

HARBOUR & EASTERN DOCKLANDS

OPENBARE BIBLIOTHEEK AMSTERDAM

Amsterdam Public Library; ☎ 523 09 00; www.oba.nl; Oosterdokskade 143; ⏲ 10am-10pm; 🚊 25/26 Muziekgebouw; ♿

This nine-storey 'tower of knowledge' redefines the public library as a social point as much as a place for reading. Big, inviting couches are scattered around every floor of the light-filled building, there are scads of free internet terminals, and the cafe on the top floor (an outlet of La Place, p50) also offers a beautiful view.

SHOP

DE ODE *Speciality Shop*

☎ 419 08 82; Levantkade 51; ⏲ by appointment only; 🚊 10 Azartplein

Send your loved ones off in style, with a creative casket from this one-of-a-kind shop. Open by appointment only, but a couple of interesting options are always on display in the window.

JC CREATIONS *Clothing*

☎ 419 72 20; Baron GA Tindalstraat 150; ⏲ 11am-6pm Tue-Fri, 11am-5pm Sat; 🚊 10 C van Eesterenlaan

Take a deep breath when you enter this small shop: classy corsets are the speciality. Plenty of ready-made options, and custom orders welcome.

KEET IN HUIS *Children's*

☎ 419 59 58; KNSM-laan 297; ⏲ Tue-Sun; 🚊 10 Azartplein

At this two-storey emporium, the young ones frolic in the play area while their superhip parents pick up Bugaboo strollers, funky room decor, nappy bags with flair and oodles of adorable clothing.

POL'S POTTEN *Design*

☎ 419 35 41; KNSM-laan 39; 🚊 10 Azartplein

How do new residents in this style-conscious district furnish their new apartments? They head straight to this large interior-design shop, which has some particularly nice ceramic work.

SISSY-BOY
Clothing, Housewares

☎ 419 15 59; KNSM-laan 19; ⏲ 9am-6pm Tue-Sat, 10am-6pm Sun & Mon; 🚊 10 Azartplein

A vast branch of the higher-end clothing-and-house-goodies chain (p47).

EAT

DE WERELDBOL
International   €

**☎ 362 87 25; Piraeusplein 59; ⏲ 5-9pm Tue-Sun; 🚊 10 Azartplein; **

A passionate and personable owner-chef, an ever-changing menu and a beautiful view of the water make this a nice place to end a day of sightseeing in this district. Note the early closing time.

🍴 EINDE VAN DE WERELD
Vegetarian €
☎ 419 02 22; opposite Javakade 4; ⏰ from 6pm Wed & Fri; 🚊 10 Azartplein; Ⓥ ♿
At the end of the world to Amsterdammers, look for the big yellow boat *Quo Vadis*. The volunteer-run onboard restaurant is cheap and very cheerful. Show up early, because you can't reserve, and when the food's gone, it's gone.

🍴 FIFTEEN *Italian* €€€
☎ 509 50 15; Jollemanhof 9; ⏰ lunch Mon-Sat, dinner daily; 🚊 25 PTA; ♿
Following 'naked chef' Jamie Oliver's model for training underprivileged youth to cook, this industrial space is fun and scrawled with graffiti. Diners all get the same four-course menu, which changes weekly. Opinions are divided on the food and the enterprise, but our meal here was tasty and well executed.

🍴 FRANK'S SMOKE HOUSE
Sandwich Shop €
☎ 670 07 74; Wittenburgergracht 303; ⏰ 9am-4pm Mon, 9am-6pm Tue-Fri, 9am-5pm Sat; 🚊 10 1e Coehoornstraat, 🚌 22/43 Wittenburgergracht

Frank has a knack for smoked eel – and salmon, halibut, tuna and much more. His little shop is primarily takeaway (you can get anything vacuum-packed, to carry through customs), but you can also sit down at the single table and have an excellent mackerel sandwich, bowl of soup or plate of charcuterie.

🍴 GARE DE L'EST
International €€
☎ 463 06 20; Cruquiusweg 9; ⏰ dinner; 🚊 4 Zeeburgerdijk, 🚌 43 Stadsdeel Zeeburg
Gare de l'Est's four chefs are as eclectic as its rich Morocco-meets-Paris interior. We sampled a Mediterranean-influenced menu (other possibilities include North African or Asian), a single four-course menu of brilliantly prepared seafood and a beautiful cheese plate. Well worth the trek.

🍴 KOMPASZAAL *Cafe* €
☎ 419 95 96; KNSM-laan 311; ⏰ 11am-1am Wed-Sun; 🚊 10 Azartplein; ♿
Set in the arrivals hall of the century-old Royal Dutch Steamboat Company (KNSM in Dutch), this cafe is a great place to have a bowl of soup or an *uitsmijter* (open-face egg sandwich) – or just a beer – while you admire the groovy green tiles and the water view from the balcony. On the ground

floor, check out the scale models of the Eastern Docklands.

🍴 ROOS EN NOOR
International €
☎ 419 14 40; Baron GA Tindalstraat 148; ⏱ 4-9pm Mon-Fri, 3-8pm Sat & Sun; 🚋 10 C van Eesterenlaan; Ⓥ

This chic little takeaway shop has a vast buffet, with prepared items like Chinese-spice duck and roasted beets, as well as full meals and sweets. It's a nice place to grab a late lunch or a sunset picnic while exploring the docklands' architecture.

🍴 SNEL *International* €€
☎ 561 36 77; Oostelijke Handelskade 34; ⏱ 7am-1am; 🚋 10 C van Eesterenlaan

We mention this restaurant not really for a full meal, but as an excuse to duck into the supremely cool Lloyd Hotel, set in the shell of a 1920s brick confection. The spacious restaurant serves snacks all day, and has a great back garden.

🍴 STAR FERRY *Cafe* €€
☎ 788 20 90; Piet Heinkade 1; ⏱ 10.30am-11pm Tue-Sun; 🚋 25/26 Muziekgebouw; ♿ Ⓥ ♨

The flash cafe at the Muziekgebouw is hard to beat for panoramic views of the harbour, especially at sunset. The food is unremarkable, but there are

delectable cakes from esteemed city bakery Holtkamp.

🍸 DRINK
🍸 KANIS & MEILAND *Cafe*
☎ 418 24 39; Levantkade 127; 🚋 10 Azartplein; ♨

As the first cafe in the neighbourhood, this roomy space has collected plenty of regulars, who sip coffee and spread out at the reading table. Outside seats take in a great view of the 'mainland'.

🍸 KHL *Cafe*
☎ 779 15 75; Oostelijke Handelskade 44; 🚋 10 C van Eesterenlaan; ♿

Just down from the Lloyd Hotel, KHL is a one-time squatter cafe gone legit. It's in a historic brick building – one of the few left in the area – and the garden is worth a glass or two. There's often eclectic music in the back room on weekends.

PLAY

BIMHUIS *Concert Hall*

☎ 788 21 88; www.bimhuis.nl; Piet Heinkade 3; tickets €12-20; 🚋 25/26 Muziekgebouw; ♿

The core of Amsterdam's influential jazz and improvisational music scene since 1973, the Bimhuis has kept its focus even after merging (architecturally) with the Muziekgebouw (right). Tuesdays at 10.30pm from September to June are an open jam session – fun and free.

CONSERVATORIUM VAN AMSTERDAM
Concert Hall

☎ 527 75 50; www.conservatorium vanamsterdam.nl; Oosterdokskade 151; 🚋 25/26 Muziekgebouw

The city's prestigious music school, set in a dramatic building on the harbour, is a great place to see jazz, opera and classical performances, at very affordable prices.

MUZIEKGEBOUW AAN 'T IJ
Concert Hall

☎ 788 20 00; www.muziekgebouw .nl; Piet Heinkade 1; tickets €8.50-27.50; 🚋 25/26 Muziekgebouw; ♿

This magnificent building plays host to everything from the Holland Symfonia (which typically

The intriguing exterior of Amsterdam's Centre for Architecture (ARCAM; p133)

backs the national ballet) to the prestigious Metropole Orkest, which does smart arrangements of jazz and pop.

⭐ PANAMA
Nightclub, Live Music
☎ 311 86 89; www.panama.nl; Oostelijke Handelskade 4; 🚊 10/26 Rietlandpark

A full schedule of themed nights and international DJs sees Panama's club packed most nights, and it also books live music and comedy. Despite the Central American name the decor is Asian. The cocktails are fantastic.

>OUTER DISTRICTS

You wouldn't know it from the postcards, but Amsterdam extends well beyond the main canal rings. The city incorporates both dense urban housing projects and fields filled with cows — and it's all a surprisingly short bike, ferry or metro ride away. The areas described in the following pages can be visited in a few hours, or a trip can take the better part of a day, depending on your interests. The city's biggest green space, Amsterdam's 'worst' neighbourhood (which also has some of its best new architecture) and the part of the city that looks remarkably like the country— none of these spots have any notable museums or other typical sights, but they're the perfect change of pace from the close confines of the historic centre. And you're sure to return with a whole new perception of Amsterdam.

Boats moored on the Amstel River

DE BIJLMER

Blij in de Bijlmer! (Happy in the Bijlmer!) read the T-shirts worn by boosters of what was just a decade ago Amsterdam's most notorious neighbourhood, known for muggings, junkies and public housing gone wrong. No part of Amsterdam has changed so dramatically in such a short time. The city's largest Surinamese population lives here, along with immigrants from west and north Africa. A beautiful lake, Gaasperplas, lies just to the south. And what used to be bleak, Le Corbusier–inspired concrete is now a playground for some of the Netherlands' most innovative architects.

It's nice, but not necessary, to visit by bike, though the 30-minute ride from the city centre isn't particularly scenic. Hop on the metro (you can bring your wheels) to the dramatic Nicholas Grimshaw–designed

Amsterdam ArenA: Ajax' high-tech home turf

Bijlmer Arena station, opened in 2007. To the west lies **Amsterdam ArenA** stadium, home of Amsterdam's revered football club, Ajax. In the shopping plaza east of the tracks, in front of the weird polygonal **ING building** (energy-efficient and 'green' in the '80s, well ahead of its time), look for the **Imagine IC** cultural centre, which dispenses excellent free audio tours of the area, as well as maps. From here, you can wind your way east, passing all kinds of novel structures, including a miniature version of the NEMO building (p133).

Eventually these give way to the few remaining '**honeycomb blocks**' of the original Bijlmer layout, each containing some 400 apartments. The 1960s brochures touted 'a modern city where the people of today can find the residential environment of tomorrow'. But the isolated, austere project rapidly lost lustre and, in the 1970s, the city began to funnel poor immigrants into the empty apartments. By the '80s, crime was common, and the infrastructure crumbling. Former residents lament the trash-filled lawns and broken elevators of those days, but many also wax nostalgic about the tight-knit community and the surrounding greenery.

In 1992 an El Al cargo plane crashed into two of the blocks, killing 43 people, many of them undocumented foreigners – a **memorial** stands in front of the missing buildings. The tragedy kick-started a re-evaluation of the neighbourhood that has shifted into wholesale rebuilding, and shifted the balance far in favour of privately owned property, rather than publicly managed apartments. Around the Kraaiennest metro stop, things still look pretty unreconstructed, except for the shiny **Taibah Mosque**, the first mosque built in the Netherlands, in 1984. The Ganzenhoef stop, due north, is a mix of old and new buildings, and home to a vibrant street market (on Saturdays) as well as a children's petting zoo, and a great Surinamese-Javanese restaurant, **De Smeltkroes**.

INFORMATION

Location 7.5km southeast of central Amsterdam
Getting there Ⓜ Bijlmer Arena, Ganzenhoef or Kraaiennest
Contact Imagine IC (☎ 489 48 66; www.imagineic.nl; Bijlmerplein 1006; ⏱ 11am-5pm Tue-Sat, 11am-9pm Thu)
Eating Kam Yin (☎ 409 58 88; Bijlmerplein 525; ⏱ 11am-9pm Mon-Sat, 3-9pm Sun), a branch of the Warmoesstraat restaurant (p50); De Smeltkroes (☎ 495 20 76; Bijlmerdreef 1289; ⏱ 10.30am-9.30pm Mon-Fri, 1-9.30pm Sat)

OUTER DISTRICTS

AMSTERDAM-NOORD

Even to most residents of Amsterdam, the north of the city is like another planet. But it's only a short ferry ride across the IJ to pretty old homes, isolated villages, open farmland and cows galore – all within the city limits. Everything's close enough for a day or afternoon bike ride; pick up a free Amsterdam-Noord map at one of the VVV (tourist board) offices at Centraal Station (p179).

Fans of derelict industry can head first for **NDSM-werf**, a shipyard that now contains art studios and a skate park. Grab a coffee at the sleek **IJ-kantine** right at the ferry pier, or the funkier **Noorderlicht**, inside the NDSM area.

Other highlights within the urban part of the Noord are the pretty homes and lush gardens that line **Stoombootweg**, on the west side, as well as **Nieuwendammerdijk** on the east, a beautiful long row of cottages with a village feel. Behind the dyke is **Nieuwendam**, an Amsterdam School housing project with winding streets and a pretty central square.

Heading north along the **Noordhollandsch Kanaal**, you'll pass a working windmill and soon be out in the country – a patchwork of fields divided by canals. You can make an easy loop around the villages of **Zunderdorp**, **Ransdorp**, **Holysloot** and **Broek in Waterland** (the last one's not technically in Amsterdam, but who's counting?). They're each only a few kilometres apart – though getting to or from Holysloot requires walking your bike across some fields and using the city's tiniest ferry.

Do pace yourself a bit as the wind is almost always against you when you turn back towards the city. If you time it right, you can finish up with dinner back at **Hotel de Goudfazant** in an industrial space directly on the IJ, and return to Centraal Station via the IJplein ferry.

INFORMATION

Location North across the IJ from Centraal Station; Broek in Waterland, the furthest village mentioned here, is 9km north

Getting there See ferry details on p174; Holysloot ferry (9.30am-5pm daily Jul-Aug, Sat & Sun only mid-Apr–May & Sep-Oct)

Eating IJ-kantine (☎ 633 71 62; www.ijkantine.nl; MT Ondinaweg 15-17; ⏱ 9am-late); Noorderlicht (☎ 492 27 70; www.noorderlichtcafe.nl, in Dutch; TT Neveritaweg 33; ⏱ 11am-late); Hotel de Goudfazant (☎ 636 15 70; www.hoteldegoudfazant.nl, in Dutch; Aambeeldstraat 10h; ⏱ 6pm-1am Tue-Sun)

AMSTERDAMSE BOS

The Amsterdam Woods is a sprawling green area, roughly 2km by 5km of trees and open fields, with cycling and walking paths. In the densest thickets you'll forget you're near a city at all (until you hear a jet overhead on its way to nearby Schiphol), and it's a wonderful place to let kids run free.

The area was laid out during the 1930s as a make-work program, and it has grown up beautifully – rare birds nest in the grasslands, and frogs croak in the marshy areas. There's a botanical garden in an area called **Vogeleiland** (Bird Island), the reeds around the **Amsterdamse Poel** harbour wild orchids and you can go fishing in the lakes (get a permit at the visitors centre).

Take young ones to **De Ridammerhoeve**, a delightful working goat farm where kids can feed bottles of milk to, well, kids. The cafeteria sells tasty goat's-milk smoothies and ice cream, as well as cheeses made on the premises. Kids can scramble around in the trees at **Fun Forest**, a network of ropes course and climbing activities for different ages and levels of nerve.

On the north side, near the main entrance, the **Bosbaan** is a long lake for sculling – you can sit and watch the rowers from yet another cafe. Or you can rent a canoe yourself and paddle through some of the wetlands. Bicycles are available at the main entrance if you don't want to ride down on your own. And if all that sounds just too active, head to **Zuiver**, an astonishing state-of-the-art indoor-outdoor sauna complex where you can easily lounge all day.

INFORMATION

Location 5.5km southwest of central Amsterdam

Getting there (🚊) 170/172 from Centraal Station; historic tram from Amsterdam Tram Museum (☎ 673 75 38; www.museumtramlijn.org; Amstelveenseweg 264; €4/2; 🕙 11am-5.30pm Sun Apr-Oct; 🚊 16); cycle through Vondelpark and south on Amstelveenseweg (45min)

Contact visitors centre (☎ 545 61 00; www.amsterdamsebos.nl; Bosbaanweg 5)

Activities bicycles per hr/day €4.50/9; canoes per hr from €6; Fun Forest (☎ 642 96 83; www.funforest.nl; Bosbaanweg 3; adult/child 8-13yr/family €21.50/16.50/19.50; 🕙 noon-6pm Wed-Fri, 10am-7pm Sat & Sun); Zuiver (☎ 301 07 10; www.spazuiver.nl; Koenenkade 8; all day/after 5pm €35/25; 🕙 10am-midnight)

When to go visitors centre (🕙 noon-5pm, park 🕙 24hr)

Eating De Ridammerhoeve (☎ 645 50 34; 🕙 10am-5pm Wed-Mon Mar-Oct, Wed-Sun Nov-Feb)

Amsterdam's historic canal houses all look roughly the same on the outside. But inside there could be a jazz jam session, a gay club night, an intimate restaurant or a supercool hotel. Snapshots is a guide to which scenes flourish behind which canal-house doors.

When a herring craving strikes, head to one of the city's traditional herring stalls

ACCOMMODATION

Amsterdam is so compact that your hotel location doesn't matter a great deal – everything's relatively accessible. That said, you might prefer the character of a specific neighbourhood. The canal ring – any address on Herengracht, Keizersgracht, Prinsengracht or Singel – is the most desirable area, both for aesthetics and quiet. The **Hotel Pulitzer** (www.luxurycollection .com/pulitzer) is the loveliest, but you can get water views for less at **Prinsenhof** (www.hotelprinsenhof.com) and **Chic & Basic** (www.chicandbasic.com), which has modern style in an old frame. The Jordaan is charming, but has very few hotels – one is **Hotel van Onna** (www.hotelvanonna.nl). These areas also hold a lot of restaurants and cafes – it's easy to get home after a decadent dinner.

Unless you're not planning to actually sleep, we don't recommend staying in De Wallen (the red-light district) or anywhere on the Damrak, where the hotels are superficially decent but usually nasty inside. Better to stay a short walk away in the Nieuwmarkt area, at a place like **Misc Eat Drink Sleep** (www.hotelmisc.nl).

The area between Vondelpark and Museumplein – with midrange places like **Hotel Piet Hein** (www.hotelpiethein.nl) or **Hotel Fita** (www.hotelfita.com) – is handy for museum-goers, though not the liveliest at night. If you prefer to look at people rather than paintings, then multicultural De Pijp is the place to be – there aren't many hotels here, but places like **Between Art & Kitsch B&B** (www.between-art-and-kitsch.com) are relatively inexpensive.

Due to a shortage of hotel rooms, doing Amsterdam on the cheap can be impossible unless you plan months in advance. If only there were more places like the impeccable **Hotel Brouwer** (www.hotelbrouwer.nl), a lovely

Need a place to stay? Find and book it at lonelyplanet.com. Over 90 properties are featured for Amsterdam – each personally visited, thoroughly reviewed and happily recommended by a Lonely Planet author. From hostels to high-end hotels, we've hunted out the places that will bring you unique and special experiences. Read independent reviews by authors and other travellers, and get practical information including amenities, maps and photos. Then reserve your room simply and securely via Hotels & Hostels – our online booking service. It's all at lonelyplanet.com/hotels.

house in the Western Canal Belt. The hip **Lloyd Hotel** (www.lloydhotel.com) also has a few bargain rooms, though its Eastern Docklands location lacks much street life. Any cheaper, though, and you risk fleapit territory. Better opt for a hostel, like the high-style **Stayokay Zeeburg** (www.stayokay.com).

Expect to pay between €22 and €40 for a hostel bed, and anywhere from €80 to €300 for a double room during the summer high season. Except at the top end, you'll never get a lot of space, nor air-conditioning, and you'll probably have to carry your luggage up perilously steep stairs.

One of the great treats in Amsterdam is staying in some creatively adapted spaces. **Amrâth** (www.amrathamsterdam.com) occupies the stunning Scheepvaarthuis, **Hotel Arena** (www.hotelarena.nl) is a converted orphanage (and another good budget option), and the **Windketel** (www.windketel.nl), a bit west of the Jordaan, lets you sleep in a converted octagonal water tower.

For deals on some of these and larger hotels, visit www.hotels.nl. Or to really feel like a local, rent an apartment. **Citymundo** (www.citymundo.com) and **Alexander's Apartments** (www.alexandersapartments.com) are reliable brokers; Citymundo offers houseboats as well, with a three-night minimum. You can also check www.expatica.com and www.craigslist.com for sublets, swaps and other options.

IF YOU LOVE...

- > **Philosophy** Hotel de Filosoof (www.hotelfilosoof.nl)
- > **Bikes** Bicycle Hotel Amsterdam (www.bicyclehotel.com)
- > **Boats** Frederic's Houseboats (www.frederic.nl)
- > **Happy hookers** Xaviera Hollander B&B (www.xavierahollander.com)
- > **Drop-dead luxury** Amstel (www.amsterdam.intercontinental.com)

TOP FIVE HIGH-STYLE HOTELS

- > College Hotel (www.thecollegehotel.nl)
- > Dylan (www.dylanamsterdam.com)
- > Lloyd Hotel (www.lloydhotel.com)
- > Park Hotel (www.parkhotel.nl)
- > Toren (www.thetoren.nl)

TOP FIVE CANAL VIEWS

- > Canal House (www.canalhouse.nl)
- > Hotel de L'Europe (www.leurope.nl)
- > Pulitzer (www.luxurycollection.com/pulitzer)
- > Seven Bridges (www.sevenbridgeshotel.nl)
- > Seven One Seven (www.717hotel.nl)

TOP FIVE SMALL GEMS

- > Collector (www.the-collector.nl)
- > Maes B&B (www.bedandbreakfastamsterdam.com)
- > Miauw Suites (www.miauw.com)
- > Orlando (www.hotelorlando.nl)
- > 't Hotel (www.thotel.nl)

FOOD

Maybe it's the centuries of trade, maybe it's the meat-and-potatoes essence of traditional Dutch fare, but Amsterdammers embrace global cuisines with zeal. Even a humble *eetcafé* (a cafe that serves casual meals) might offer Indonesian satay, Moroccan couscous and Indian curry on its menu – all with a side of *frites* (French fries), of course. On any given night, you can eat Ethiopian, Thai or South African, but the most popular foreign cuisine is spicy Indonesian – the multiple-plate *rijsttafel* (rice table) is a Dutch invention.

The city's finer restaurants take inspiration from France, but they work with local produce, fish from the North Sea and lamb from the island of Texel. The result is uniquely Dutch – a potato salad with smoked eel at Greetje (p128) for instance, or a perfectly cooked piece of venison at Marius (p78). But as much as the Dutch mock their own cuisine, the places that stick to tradition can also be deeply satisfying. On a drizzly day, nothing hits the spot like a steak at Loetje (p101), or a big bowl of thick pea soup at Moeders (p70).

One distinct element of the Amsterdam dining scene is the large number of restaurants that serve only one or two set menus per night. Submitting to the whims of a chef can get you fresh-from-the-garden gourmet at De Kas (p117), international elegance at Gare de l'Est (p137) or casual camaraderie at Balthazar's Keuken (p68). Even restaurants that do a broader menu also offer one or two fixed-price three-course menus, which can be excellent value.

Dinner in Amsterdam can require a bit of planning. Aside from *eetcafés,* nearly every restaurant takes reservations, and any place with a bit of buzz will require a call at least a couple of days ahead. It never hurts to call a restaurant to reserve, even just a few hours early. Moreover, restaurants typically do only one seating per night. Amsterdammers dine relatively early, and once they sit down, they're at the table for the better part of the evening.

The midday meal, on the other hand, is usually a modest affair. The Dutch are quite fond of their cheese sandwiches, and haven't really taken to 'doing lunch'. There's no shortage of charming cafes in which to have a light bite, but some of the best bets are the spartan *broodje* (sandwich) shops like Van Dobben (p90) or Dop (p48) that serve white rolls with butter and thinly sliced meat.

Speaking of meat, vegetarians are generally well cared-for, with at least one meatless option on the menu just about anywhere you go. And there are a number of excellent all-vegetarian restaurants as well.

A note on service, an endless source of dismay for visitors and Dutch diners alike: yes, your waiter or waitress may often be distracted, or grumpy or forgetful. Just try to forget it and chalk it up to cultural difference – it's never personal. Etiquette demands that you must ask for your bill when you're ready to leave – the staff will never bring it unrequested, lest it appear they're trying to rush you.

BEST SWEET TREATS
> **Chocolate and cakes** Unlimited Delicious (p73)
> **Fancy lollies** Papabubble (p67)
> **Ice cream** IJscuypje (p110)
> **Stroopwafels** Lanskroon (p50)
> **Liquorice and more** Het Oude-Hollandsche Snoepwinkeltje (p66)

BEST BITES
> **Roast-beef sandwich** Van Dobben (p90)
> **Fries with Belgian mayo** Vlaams Frites Huis (p53)
> **Loempias** Albert Cuypmarkt (p106)
> **Fresh herring sandwich** Rob Wigboldus Vishandel (p51)
> **Aged gouda** De Kaaskamer (p69)

Top left Sample breads of the world at the Noordermarkt (p67) in the Jordaan

ARCHITECTURE

It's impossible not to be struck by Amsterdam's well-preserved beauty; the lovely canalscapes depicted in centuries-old paintings are remarkably unchanged. Historian Geert Mak once described Amsterdam as 'a Cinderella under glass', spared from wartime destruction and, for the most part, ham-fisted developers. The gracious old centre has no fewer than 7000 historical monuments, more humpback bridges than Venice and more trees per capita than Paris.

At first glance, the narrow buildings all look the same. But details like gables (decorations at roof-level) give clues to age: a simple pointed gable is the oldest, dating from the late 16th century, while steps ruled the 17th, and curvy bell gables were fashionable in the 18th.

You'll also notice that more recent constructions have been wedged in between these Golden Age relics. Many of the newer buildings – also brick, so they blend in – are from the early 20th century, in a style known as Amsterdam School (boxed text, p106). Visit masterpieces like the Scheepvaarthuis (p125), and also look at the canal bridges, especially along Leidsestraat, trimmed in winding wrought iron and odd animals. Even the shell-shaped green pissoirs around the city are Amsterdam School designs.

All the interesting new construction is on Amsterdam's fringes. Orient yourself first with a visit to the city planning exhibit at the Zuiderkerk (p125), then make the trek from the warren of the medieval centre out to the spacious Eastern Docklands (p132). Both areas have canals, but otherwise, they're worlds apart. In the harbour, the green ship-shaped NEMO (p133), built in 1997, is already a classic, while the 2007 OBA (Amsterdam Public Library; p136) next door redefines the public library. The Muziekgebouw aan 't IJ (p139) is oriented purely towards the water. For even more inventive new building, visit the Bijlmer neighbourhood (p142), where architecture's effect on community is patently clear.

No matter what your architectural tastes, stop in at ARCAM (p133), the city architecture museum that is itself an ingenious structure. There's an excellent timeline showcasing the city's building history downstairs. The enthusiastic staff can recommend areas of the city to explore, and also run periodic tours around the city.

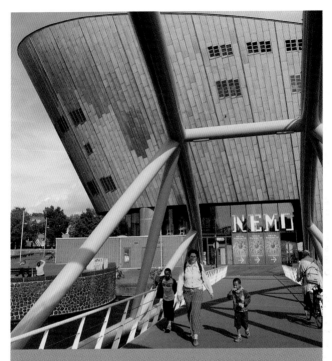

TOP ARCHITECTURAL ICONS
> Westerkerk (p63)
> Rijksmuseum (p98)
> NEMO (p133)
> Het Schip (p78)
> Beurs van Berlage
  (p41)

TOP INTERIORS
> Tuschinskitheater
  (p85)
> Koninklijk Paleis (p42)
> Museum Van Loon (p84)
> Rembrandthuis (p124)
> Oude Kerk (p43)

Above Set sail for one of Amsterdam's modern architectural icons, NEMO (p133), in the Eastern Docklands

KIDS

Never mind the sex and drugs – Amsterdam is a children's paradise. The small scale, the quirky buildings, the lack of car traffic and the canals all combine to make it a wondrous place for little ones. And the Dutch seem to always be dreaming up new ways to entertain children. Whether that's a hands-on science museum like NEMO (p133), a free puppet show on Dam Square (p41) or simply a kid-oriented tour through the Rembrandthuis (p124) or Ons' Lieve Heer op Solder (p43), the goal is to keep kids occupied and intrigued, so their parents can relax a little and enjoy themselves too. In fact, most of the major museums offer a kids' tour, and the Rijksmuseum (p98) is free for under-18s.

While you're at the NEMO (and you have to go, if only for the building – it's big and green and funny-looking, and the rooftop deck is a great spot for looking down on the city's medieval centre), be sure to visit the adjacent *Amsterdam* ship, with all its cubbyholes and a rambunctious, piratelike crew. Teens who've read *The Diary of Anne Frank* will certainly want to visit Anne Frank Huis (p62), but if you need to entertain kids of all ages, Tropenmuseum (p113) has enough colourful stuff from all over the world to impress everyone (including adults).

Kids often just need room to run around. That's easily found at Vondelpark (p99), in particular at Het Groot Melkhuis, a cafe adjoining a packed playground. Or make a day of it and head out to Amsterdamse Bos (p145) to the adorable goat farm where kids can feed and pet the animals.

Dining out is a little more limited – a lot of restaurants are quite small and quiet and have a romantic atmosphere. But anywhere that calls itself an *eetcafé* is casual enough not to mind smaller diners, and we especially recommend Loetje (p101), Bazar (p109) and Los Pilones (p70). Otherwise consider combining a free ferry ride with dinner at kid-friendly IJ-kantine at NDSM-werf (p144). In summertime, treat kids to *poffertjes* (minipancakes sprinkled with powdered sugar) at temporary stands (there's a circus-themed one just off the Leidseplein near Stadhouderskade); in winter, they're replaced with *oliebollen* (deep-fried proto-doughnuts). Little ones also love big Dutch-style pancakes – the tiny Pannenkoekenhuis Upstairs (p51) has a fairy-tale feel, and Pancakes! (p70) has a huge menu.

High-end hotels often offer baby-sitting services. To arrange your own, contact **Oppascentrale Kriterion** (Map pp122-3, D6; ☎ 624 58 48; www.oppascentrale kriterion.nl, in Dutch; Roetersstraat 170), the best known in town – but you need to register ahead of time and pay a nominal joining fee.

TOP KIDS' ACTIVITIES
> Ice skating at Museumplein (p96)
> Canal-boat rides (p178)
> Ferry across the IJ (p175)
> Eating pancakes (p70)
> TunFun (p131)

TOP KIDS' SIGHTS
> Amsterdamse Bos (p145)
> Artis Zoo (p121)
> NEMO (p133)
> Tropenmuseum (p113)
> Vondelpark (p99)

Top left A small child takes in the city's atmosphere from the comfort of a *bakfiets* (cargo bike; p16)

SNAPSHOTS

SHOPPING

Amsterdam is filled with tiny speciality shops that seem to exist outside the laws of supply and demand. Shops stocked with nothing but buttons, beads or bowties may not be for you, but at some point, you'll turn a corner and see the store that specialises in precisely the thing you've been hunting for – whether you knew it or not.

Each neighbourhood has a different consumer character. In the Centrum, the long pedestrian strip formed by Kalverstraat and Nieuwendijk (Map pp38–9, B8-D3) has more H&M branches than you can count, plus there are large bookstores on the Spui. Over in De Wallen, the displays in the sex shops can cause serious whiplash. But just where the glow from the red lights fades, the Zeedijk (Map pp38–9, E4) has a string of lovely boutiques, alternating with long-established bars and Chinese groceries, and Oude Hoogstraat and Nieuwe Hoogstraat (Map pp38–9, D6-E6) offer another strip of eclectic shops.

On the west side, Haarlemmerstraat and Haarlemmerdijk (Map pp60-61, C1-F3) are lined with hip boutiques and food shops, while just to the south, the Negen Straatjes (p14) are ground zero for quirky shopkeepers. But don't blow your budget before poking around in the neighbouring Jordaan, an area known for its vintage goodies. Dust and clutter can disguise amazing gems, though proprietors almost always know the value of their finds. Centuries of savvy trading made this city great, after all.

There's less dust and far more valuable stuff in the Spiegelkwartier antiques district, the area along Spiegelgracht and Nieuwe Spiegelstraat in the Southern Canal Belt (Map pp82–3, C4). If you need the perfect 18th-century *objet* for the mantel in your country estate, come here first.

The city's modern luxury shopping street is Pieter Cornelisz Hooftstraat (Map p97, E2), with the obligatory Dolce & Gabbana and the like. Even if you're not in the market for a Vuitton bag, this street is interesting from an anthropological perspective: conspicuous consumption is generally frowned upon in Amsterdam, and these are the only few blocks where it appears to flourish. More genteel shoppers in the Old South head to pretty Cornelis Schuytstraat (Map p97, D3), off Vondelpark.

But once you find your dream item, be ready to pay cash – a surprising number of businesses don't take credit cards.

BEST HOUSEWARES
> Droog (p126)
> Frozen Fountain (p65)
> & Klevering (p64)
> Wonderwood (p47)
> HEMA (p45)

BEST FASHION
> Van Ravenstein (p68)
> Young Designers United (p86)
> Marlies Dekkers (p100)
> Hester van Eeghen (p66)
> Sprmrkt (p68)

BEST GIFTS
> **T-shirt** Mark Raven Grafiek (p46)
> **Chocolates** Unlimited Delicious (p73)
> **Felt clogs** Shirdak (p67)
> **Bike seat cover** Kitsch Kitchen (p66)
> **Enamel 'zuiker' (sugar) pot** De Emaillekeizer (p108)

BEST ANTIQUES & VINTAGE
> Waterloopleinmarkt (p127)
> Laura Dols (p67)
> De Looier (p65)
> Bebob Design (p85)
> Brilmuseum (p64)

Top left and **Above** Amsterdam's markets offer clothing, jewellery, food and almost everything in between

GAY & LESBIAN

To call Amsterdam a gay capital still doesn't express just how welcoming and open the scene is here. After all, this is the city that gave the world *Butt* magazine. It's also the city that claims to have founded the world's first gay and lesbian bar, 't Mandje (p56) – an obligatory stop on any Zeedijk cruise. It's also the city that hosts one of the world's largest and most flamboyant Pride parades, and certainly the only one that takes place on boats (p24).

Amsterdam's gay scene is a diverse one, with the Warmoesstraat perhaps the most notorious district, known for its numerous leather bars and darkrooms. Reguliersdwarsstraat is the polar opposite, all air-kissing and tight T-shirts – but there's plenty of action here too. Lesbians aren't quite so visible, but have several excellent bars to choose from – Vivela-vie (p91) probably has the hottest crowd. The younger gay and lesbian subculture is more mixed, as at the come-one-come-all Getto (p54) in De Wallen, and the monthly party U.N.K. at Club 8 (p75), which is heavy on the electro and '80s-inspired fashion.

For more info – and the lowdown on many more gay and lesbian hangouts than this book can cover – visit the **Pink Point** (Map pp60-1, D5; ☾ noon-6pm Mar-Aug, limited hours Sep-Feb) on the Keizersgracht, behind the Westerkerk. Part information kiosk, part souvenir shop, it's a good place to get details on parties and social groups, and pick up a copy of the very candid *Bent Guide*.

MUSEUMS

Amsterdam's Rembrandt-crammed Rijksmuseum (p98) is currently only partially open while it undergoes renovations, but consider it a blessing in disguise: your time is freed up to visit all the other beautiful, intimate and sometimes odd collections in town. Naturally, there's that collection of work by the Netherlands' *other* famous painter, the Van Gogh Museum (p98), not to mention displays of contemporary Saudi art (p81) and cats (p84).

Some grand canal houses are dedicated to some very special interests, such as the Bijbels Museum (p62), where you can see a hand-carved scale model of the Ark of the Covenant and other 19th-century oddities, and the Tassenmuseum Hendrikje (p85), a temple of handbags. A smaller waterside house contains Ons' Lieve Heer op Solder (p43), a Catholic church hidden in the upper floors, complete with an organ, while the luxurious yet cosy Museum Van Loon (p84) feels like the inhabitants just stepped out.

But visiting museums doesn't mean you'll be poking around in dusty old rooms full of artefacts. Both the Verzetsmuseum (p125), which focuses on the Resistance in WWII, and the Amsterdams Historisch Museum (p40) use sound and video clips to great effect. The massive Tropenmuseum (p113) is an utterly absorbing tour of the Netherlands' former colonies and beyond. At the Rembrandthuis (p124) staff demonstrate crafts and printmaking techniques, and on the *Amsterdam* ship, moored next to NEMO (p133), scruffy sailors sing sea shanties. The ship actually belongs to the Scheepvaartmuseum (p133), another collection that will probably be closed while you're here. But don't worry – with all the other museums to see, you'll never miss this one.

The Rijksmuseum (p10), located in Amsterdam's museum district

GEZELLIGHEID

This particularly Dutch quality is one of the best reasons to visit Amsterdam. It's variously translated as snug, friendly, cosy, informal, companionable and convivial, but *gezelligheid* – the state of being *gezellig* – is something more easily experienced than defined. There's a sense of time stopping, an intimacy of the here and now that leaves all your troubles behind, at least until tomorrow.

You can get that warm, fuzzy feeling in many situations, but the easiest place is at a traditional *bruin café*. So-called 'brown cafes', covered in wood panelling and stained with centuries of tobacco smoke, practically have *gezelligheid* on tap, alongside the usual beer. (And why *are* the beer glasses so small here? You guessed it: more *gezellig*.) There's usually a reading table strewn with newspapers, where a couple of regulars sip their coffee and occasionally debate the issues. If the cafe cat strolls by and wants to be scratched, so much the better. By night, the golden lights come on and the beer flows freely. The oldest-school *bruin cafés* have no music, and encourage customers to toss their peanut shells on the floor.

You can also get into the *gezellig* mood at airier cafes with a pretty view, or any restaurant after dinner, where you're welcome to lounge and chat after your meal (*natafelen*, or, in Dutch, 'after-table-ing') while the candles burn low – and there are *always* candles.

Identifying the most *gezellig* spots seems a little too arbitrary – but these are some spots where we know *gezelligheid* can be found.

GEZELLIG BARS
> De Zotte (p74)
> 't Arendsnest (p76)
> 't Mandje (p56)
> 't Smalle (p77)
> Welling (p102)

GEZELLIG CAFES & RESTAURANTS
> De Jaren (p47)
> Festina Lente (p69)
> Kapitein Zeppo's (p50)
> Latei (p55)
> Van Kerkwijk (p52)

SMOKING

Even for those who don't smoke marijuana, Amsterdam's capitalist approach to soft drugs is fascinating. With menus as detailed as wine lists, 'coffeeshops' sell prerolled joints in handy plastic cases. 'Smart shops' deal in organic uppers and natural hallucinogens: counter staff advise on the nuances of dosages and possible trips, as if at a pharmacy.

Skip the generic coffeeshops with the *Pulp Fiction* soundtrack on repeat and head instead to one of the mosaic-bedecked branches of Greenhouse (p111). Newbies will like friendly Abraxas (p53), minimalist Kadinsky (p55) is for nonhippy smokers, La Tertulia (p74) is wholesome, and Rokerij (p91) is a feast for the eyes. Or you could pop into a random coffeeshop in a residential neighbourhood – usually generic, but barely distinguishable from a corner bar.

A good budtender can suggest a smoke for your tastes and won't make you buy more than a gram of anything. You're not obliged to buy weed to sit in a coffeeshop and smoke, but do pick something from the menu – nice places have all kinds of stoner-friendly treats. They'll also have pipes, bongs and vaporisers you can use.

Etiquette demands that you smoke only in coffeeshops, weed-friendly bars or secluded parts of parks. Obligatory warnings: marijuana is exceptionally strong here, so start slow. Please also listen to the experts who sell 'truffles' (the legal alternative to magic mushrooms); every year, emergency-room nurses have to sit with people on bad trips brought on by consuming more than the recommended dosage. Finally, it seems obvious, but don't buy drugs on the street. Not only are they counterfeit, but the sellers often attempt to lure would-be buyers down dark alleys and rob them – some of the only drug-related crime in Amsterdam.

The grass is always greener in Amsterdam

DRINKING & NIGHTLIFE

Though it has a wanton reputation, Amsterdam is not an all-night city, and in fact some of the most delightful drinking options – such as Brouwerij 't IJ (p129) and Wynand Fockink (p56) – kick you out just as the sun is setting. But that doesn't mean Amsterdammers don't know how to party.

That party starts at all manner of bars: *gezellig* brown cafes (p160), chic lounges where DJs spin and bartenders concoct mixed drinks, or specialists in Belgian beer. Visit sedate *proeflokalen* (tasting houses) for *jenever* (Dutch-style gin) and flavoured liqueurs, usually distilled on the premises. They're served in fluted glasses filled to the brim – bend over and slurp your first taste.

The club scene is massive – Holland gave the world Tiësto and gabber, after all. International names drop in all the time and there are extended parties like 5 Days Off (p22) and Amsterdam Dance Event (p25). At the city's many casual clubs, it really *is* all about the music – velvet ropes and VIP rooms are relatively rare. Check out record shops for party flyers and ticket presales.

The city's numerous multipurpose arts centres are one of its finest assets. At places like the Melkweg (p94), Studio K (p118) and De Badcuyp (p111), you can eat a meal, see a movie, hear a band and probably see some art on the walls. And once the bands stop, club music takes over. Funkier squats (many now legalised) such as OT301 (p103) and Zaal 100 (p75) have an even more freewheeling agenda.

BEST BARS FOR...
> **A view** Canvas op de 7e (p118)
> **An eclectic crowd** Schuim (p56)
> **Belgian beer** De Zotte (p74)
> **Cocktails** Door 74 (p91)
> **Jenever** Wynand Fockink (p56)

BEST CLUBS
> Air (p92)
> Club 8 (p75)
> Paradiso (p94)
> Studio K (p118)
> Sugar Factory (p95)

MULTICULTURALISM

Scratch that vision of a metropolis of 6ft-tall blond people. With nearly half of its population hailing from other countries, Amsterdam rivals much bigger cities for diversity. People from the Netherlands' former colonies, Indonesia and Suriname, form the largest minority groups, and the other significant presences in the city are Turks and Moroccans, many second-generation. The remaining 170 or so nationalities recorded in the census represent the rest of the globe.

Amsterdam has its share of racial and cultural issues (which came to a head in 2004, when filmmaker Theo van Gogh was murdered by a young Dutch-Moroccan), but it is remarkably integrated compared with some other European capitals. Immigrants aren't relegated to suburbs (just walk around De Pijp to hear five or 10 languages spoken), and pop Dutch movies like *Shouf Shouf Habibi* (p171) pack in the crowds. Amsterdam's multiracial character is a point of pride and, post-Theo, many Amsterdammers have scoffed at nationalist politicians such as MP Geert Wilders, the firebrand who likened the Quran to *Mein Kampf*.

And Amsterdammers always seem ready to bond over commerce – the wildly diverse Albert Cuypmarkt (p106) and Dappermarkt (p113) are two fantastic places to see this in action. For a deeper tour of Amsterdam's immigrant heritage, make a trip to the Bijlmer (p142), a housing project with a rich past. Then check out what's on at multicultural venues like De Badcuyp (p111) or Podium Mozaïek (see boxed text, p75) to hear what Amsterdam's future will sound like.

MUSIC

Amsterdam fosters music geeks. Similar to the city's niche shops, there's a fervent subculture for just about every genre – just hang out near your favourite albums at Concerto (p85) and you'll soon be swapping trivia with fellow fans. There's a particularly hot avant-garde improvisational music scene in small venues like Zaal 100 (boxed text, p75) and grand ones like Bimhuis (p139), a sleek new concert hall on the IJ that carries the spirit of a much older, funkier club inside it.

If that's too geeky for you, hit one of the more traditional jazz clubs. In the city where Chet Baker met his end, you can see a live combo every night of the week. Two stalwarts are Jazz Café Alto (p93), where fusion saxophonist Hans Dulfer takes to the stage every Wednesday, and De Engelbewaarder (p130), for its long-running Sunday session. Visiting musicians usually play at Bimhuis.

Classical fans will also be delighted by Amsterdam, with the flawless Concertgebouw (p102) or the dramatic Muziekgebouw aan 't IJ (p139) to choose from. Lunchtime concerts and student shows at the Conservatorium van Amsterdam (p139) are often free.

The city's dance music scene thrives as well, with DJs catering to nearly every taste – see Drinking & Nightlife (p162) for club recommendations. Local rock doesn't have much notoriety beyond the now-deceased Herman Brood, who burned out rather than faded away, but huge touring names often play smallish venues like Melkweg (p94) and Paradiso (p94). It's a treat to catch one of your favourites here.

A local band offers a tune to the masses visiting Noordermarkt (p67)

The old and the new: traditional gable on the left, modern building by Mart van Schijndel on the right

BACKGROUND
HISTORY
FROM THE BEGINNING
The region that spawned a giant trading community was originally an in-hospitable patchwork of lakes, swamps and peat. The oldest archaeological finds here date from the Roman Empire, but the first settlement was not until around 1200, when a fishing community known as Aemstelre-damme – 'the dam across the Amstel River' – emerged at what is now the Dam (p41). On 27 October 1275, the count of Holland (Holland being the name of the surrounding territory) waived tolls on locks and bridges for those who lived around the dam, and the town of Amsterdam was born.

EARLY TRADE
Although the earliest settlers focused on fishing, it was commercial trade – particularly in beer, an essential commodity at a time when water wasn't clean enough to drink – that soon put Holland on the map. Amsterdam muscled into the North and Baltic Seas, sending *vrijbuiters* (booty-chasers), with their holds full of cloth and salt to exchange for grain and timber, to crack the German Hanseatic League that ruled the trade routes. By the late 1400s, nearly two-thirds of ships sailing to and from the Baltic Sea were from Holland, and most were based in Amsterdam. The original harbour on the Damrak and Rokin was extended north into the IJ river, near what is now Centraal Station. Canals were dug to the warehouses in today's medieval centre. Unfettered by high taxes and medieval feudal structures, Amsterdam fostered a society of individualism and capitalism.

INDEPENDENT REPUBLIC
The Protestant Reformation of the 15th century spawned a doctrine espoused by French theologian John Calvin. Stern and austere, Calvinism became an integral element in the struggle of the Low Countries (as Belgium, Luxembourg and the Netherlands were known) against the decadent Catholic reign of Spain's Philip II and the Inquisition. In 1578 Calvinists captured Amsterdam and soon declared the northern prov-inces the independent Dutch Republic of the Seven United Netherlands, with Holland (and Amsterdam) at its core. The Calvinist ascension was tactfully called the 'Alteration', and business carried on as usual.

GOLDEN AGE

When trading rival Antwerp was retaken by the Spaniards in the late 16th century, merchants, skippers and artisans flocked to Amsterdam, and a new moneyed society emerged. The world's first regular newspaper was printed here in 1618. Persecuted Jews from Portugal and Spain also fled to Amsterdam; they knew of trade routes to the West and East Indies, introduced the diamond industry and made Amsterdam a tobacco centre. Founded in 1602, the Vereenigde Oost-Indische Compagnie (VOC, or Dutch East India Company) wrested the Asian spice trade from the Portuguese and took hold of the islands that would later be called Indonesia. By the late 17th century, the VOC was the world's richest corporation, with more than 50,000 employees and a private army.

Meanwhile the city kept pace and the population quadrupled in just a century, to 220,000 in 1700. Amsterdam became home to Europe's largest shipbuilding industry and, as wages remained low, investment flowed in. A less profitable West India Company established plantations in South America and the trading post of New Amsterdam. In a 1651 deal with the British, the Dutch chose to keep Guyana (later Suriname), and give up its northern territory – the British renamed it New York. Two decades later, Louis XIV of France invaded the Low Countries, and the brief era known as the Dutch Golden Age ended.

DECLINING FORTUNES

By the late 17th century, Dutch merchants began to invest their fortunes in secure ventures, rather than daring sea voyages and innovation. The result was stagnation, and the decline in trade brought poverty; exceptionally cold winters, especially in 1740 and 1763, froze supply boats in the river and led to serious food shortages. The mighty VOC went bankrupt in 1800, not long after the French revolutionary forces invaded the Dutch Republic. In 1806, it became a monarchy, an event soon followed by Napoleon Bonaparte's brother, Louis, occupying the city hall on the Dam with the declaration *Ik ben u konijn!* (I am your rabbit!) – he'd meant to say *koning* (king). Napoleon soon dismissed him and annexed the region into the French Empire. Amsterdam's great trade and fishing industries ground to a halt, and the city lapsed into a sleepy market town. Napoleon was defeated in 1813, opening the door for the House of Orange-Nassau to establish the United Kingdom of the Netherlands. But Amsterdam's trade with the world recovered slowly – the British had since come to dominate the seas.

GROWTH & DEPRESSION

Amsterdam shook off its torpor when the Netherlands' first rail line was inaugurated here in 1839. Major infrastructure projects such as an expanded harbour helped the city benefit from the Industrial Revolution. As the city again attracted immigrants, speculators hastily erected tenement blocks. In 1889, Centraal Station was built, its position on the IJ symbolically severing Amsterdam's historical ties with the sea. The Netherlands remained neutral in WWI, but Amsterdam's trade with the East Indies suffered because of naval blockades. Following riots over food shortages, an attempt to bring the socialist revolution to the Netherlands was halted by loyalist troops.

After the war the Netherlands focused on rebuilding its industrial base, with rapid success. Amsterdam's NDSM (Dutch Dock and Shipbuilding Company) operated the world's second-largest wharf. KLM (Royal Aviation Company) began the world's first regular air service in 1920 between Amsterdam and London, from an airstrip south of the city, and bought many of its planes from the factory of aviation pioneer Anthony Fokker to the north of the IJ. There were two huge breweries, a sizeable clothing industry and even a local car factory, and the city hosted the Olympic Games in 1928. But the global Depression of the 1930s hit Amsterdam hard. Make-work projects did little to defuse the mounting tensions between socialists, communists and a small but vocal fascist party.

WWII

When Germany invaded the Netherlands in May 1940, Amsterdammers experienced war firsthand for the first time in almost 400 years. In February 1941, dockworkers led a protest strike over the treatment of Jews. But it was already too late. Of Amsterdam's 90,000 Jews, only 5000 survived the war, the lowest proportion of anywhere in Western Europe. Canadian troops liberated the city in May 1945, but not before thousands of people had starved or frozen to death in the previous months, known as the 'Hunger Winter'.

POSTWAR CHANGE

Shortly after the war, Indonesia gained independence. US aid and newly discovered natural-gas fields helped make up for lost profits during the war years, and the city began to grow again. Massive apartment blocks were constructed to meet the continued demand for housing. By the 1960s, these were often reserved for 'guest workers' from Morocco and Turkey, who filled jobs in the industrial sectors.

By the end of the '60s, Amsterdam became Europe's 'Magic Centre'. hippies smoked dope on the Dam, camped in Vondelpark and tripped at clubs like the Melkweg, an abandoned dairy barn. In 1972 the first coffeeshop opened and in 1976 marijuana was decriminalised, to free up police resources for combating hard drugs. With soaring housing prices, squatters began to occupy buildings left empty by speculators; in the process, they helped save several notable historic structures from demolition. Historic preservation became a citywide issue in the early 1980s, when plans for a metro line and city hall complex in the old Jewish neighbourhood brought protesters to the streets.

AMSTERDAM TODAY

Since the 1990s, squatting has become more subdued and the city's economy has shifted to white-collar jobs, a thriving service industry and increasing gentrification. The ethnic make-up has changed too, with non-Dutch nationalities comprising over 45% of the population. In the first years of the 21st century, a noisy debate erupted over the Netherlands' policy towards migrants. Right-wing (and flamboyantly gay) MP candidate Pim Fortuyn transfixed the country in 2002 when he declared Holland 'full', then died from an assassin's bullet before elections. His killer wasn't a Muslim he'd condemned for homophobia, but an animal-rights activist angered by his stance on mink farming. In the autumn of 2004, outspoken filmmaker Theo van Gogh, also known for his anti-Islamic views, was shot and stabbed to death on an Amsterdam street. The killer was a young Muslim, born and raised in the Netherlands. The government swiftly mounted a unity campaign called 'We Amsterdammers', which appears to have pulled the populace together. City residents have since turned their attention to a new metro line, massive artificial islands and other grand urban projects. A rare optimism even reigned, briefly, until the global crash of 2009. Though projects continue forward, there's fresh anxiety in the city as the country's politics move to the right.

LIFE AS AN AMSTERDAMMER

Freewheeling Amsterdam is often praised for its tolerance and open-mindedness. Soft drugs, sex, nudity, eccentric behaviour – it's all met with a wry smile and a shrug, a blasé attitude developed over centuries of seeing the world flow in and out of this trading port. In fact, many *mokums* (slang for Amsterdam natives, from the Yiddish name for the city, Groot Mokum) are not just tolerant, but actively proud of the red-light district and the blatant mix of sex and industry that it represents. Gay marriage (legalised in 2001) and doctor-assisted suicide (euthanasia; permitted since 1993) are treated with the same approach. The old Calvinist streak comes out only in a dislike of attention-seeking behaviour: 'Act normal – that's crazy enough' is a common expression.

Some visitors think this means that Amsterdam is a nonstop drug-fuelled orgy. If anything, it's a nonstop *koffie verkeerd* (milky coffee) on a sunny terrace while chatting with a friend. A typical Amsterdammer has never set foot in a coffeeshop, and if they've tried marijuana, it was probably while they were on holiday in Australia. As for the red-light district, the city estimates that only 5% of customers are Dutch nationals.

Likewise, many Dutch people don't care much about the impression they make – at least beyond the polite routine of three cheek-kisses. They dress casually and comfortably (all the better for bicycling). They push to the head of the queue. And they speak their minds, often to the point of being shockingly blunt.

The cherished Dutch tolerance has also revealed its negative side. Tolerating something is in fact quite different from accepting it, say young people of Moroccan and Turkish descent. Though they're native-born citizens of the Netherlands, some ethnic Dutch still dismiss them as *allochtonen* ('out-landers'). Following some uncharacteristically divisive political debate, the Netherlands seems to be growing more conservative, favouring a Christian coalition government, restricting immigration and casting a critical eye. But this city of roughly 750,000 has largely remained staunchly left wing, looking instead to the needs of its own diverse citizens, 28% of whom are second-generation immigrants. At the heart of it, this is another element of their city that Amsterdammers are – and always will be – very proud of.

FURTHER READING

The most accessible and entertaining history of the city is *Amsterdam: A Brief Life of the City*, by Geert Mak. It combines broad historical narrative with anecdotes about Amsterdam's more riveting characters over the centuries. Mak, one of the country's leading journalists, does not shy away from depicting uncomfortable truths, be it in trade, war, religion or government. Another excellent history is Simon Schama's *The Embarrassment of*

Riches, an account of Dutch culture in the Golden Age. Schama also ties the Calvinist culture to modern Dutch society, and often turns to analysis of art – you'll learn a lot about breakfast paintings – to mirror a nation with all its neuroses and religious idiosyncrasies. Ian Buruma's *Murder in Amsterdam: Liberal Europe, Islam and the Limits of Tolerance* is a rather personal approach to the immigration debates and the death of Theo van Gogh, whom Buruma knew well.

Little Dutch fiction has made it into English, with the exception of Harry Mulisch's *De Aanslag* (The Assault), a devastating novel linking the tragedies of WWII with Cold War–era nuclear fears. Mulisch's rival, Amsterdam-born Gerard Reve, was notorious for his depiction of gay sex, often with caustic humour, and he never met a religious symbol that he didn't desecrate. None of his work is translated but his novel *De Vierde Man* (The Fourth Man) was made into a film by Paul Verhoeven in 1983.

On a more practical note, if you're a food fan, pick up a copy of Johannes van Dam's *Delicious Amsterdam,* a list of a hundred recommended restaurants (not entirely up-to-date) and a handy list of Dutch food words, for maximising your bakery time.

FILMS

Check out these films for insights into Dutch society – and scenic shots of Amsterdam. (We're specifically not recommending *Amsterdamned,* the silly 1987 thriller – the canal chase scenes were shot in Utrecht!)

De Aanslag (The Assault; 1986; Fons Rademakers). A physician spends his adult life investigating why his neighbours betrayed his family in WWII. Based on a best-selling novel by Harry Mulisch (above) and nominated for an Academy Award.

Interview (2003; Theo van Gogh). One of Van Gogh's more subdued films, in which a war correspondent conducts an interview with a soap-opera actress. An American remake was released in 2007.

Shouf Shouf Habibi (Hush Hush Baby; 2004; Albert ter Heerdt). A comedy about a Moroccan family finding its way in Dutch society, which takes a cynical look at the integration issue without taking sides.

Simon (2004; Eddy Terstall). A complicated friendship develops when a hetero hash dealer hits a gay man with his car. Simon is a pitch-perfect old-guard Jordaan native, and the film explores all the major social debates – drugs, gay rights, euthanasia – with humour.

Zus & So (2001; Paula van der Oest). A comedy about three sisters who plot to sabotage the engagement of their gay brother for material gain. Also Oscar-nominated.

Zwartboek (Black Book; 2006; Paul Verhoeven). This action-packed story explores some of the less heroic aspects of the Dutch resistance in WWII. The highest-grossing film in Dutch history, it launched the international career of today's hottest Dutch actress, Carice van Houten.

DIRECTORY
TRANSPORT
ARRIVAL & DEPARTURE
AIR

Amsterdam's **Schiphol International Airport** (☎ 794 08 00; www.schiphol.nl), 18km southwest of the city centre, is Europe's fourth-largest airport. There's a left-luggage office as well as lockers (from €5 per day). Several low-cost carriers serve **Eindhoven Airport** (☎ 022-700 07 67; www .eindhovenairport.com), 121km south of Amsterdam.

TRAIN

National and international trains arrive at Amsterdam Centraal Station (Map pp38–9, E2). Intercity trains run every 20 minutes from Den Haag (one hour) and Rotterdam (one hour); the fast Fyra runs hourly from Rotterdam (40 minutes). From Berlin, there are six day trains (six hours), requiring one transfer, and one direct night train (nine hours). Six trains run from Frankfurt (four hours). From Hamburg, there's one night train (10 hours); day trains require two transfers, with five hours' travel time. The high-speed Thalys runs from Paris (3½ hours) via Brussels at least eight times a day. Coming from London (six hours) on the Eurostar requires a transfer in Brussels; there are seven departures daily.

See www.ns.nl for national schedules and booking; www .nshispeed.nl for international booking; and www.eurostar.com for London.

BUS

Eurolines (www.eurolines.com) connects Amsterdam with all major European capitals. Buses arrive at Amstelstation, south of the centre, with an easy metro link to Centraal Station.

CLIMATE CHANGE & TRAVEL

Travel – especially air travel – is a significant contributor to global climate change. At Lonely Planet, we believe that all who travel have a responsibility to limit their personal impact. As a result, we have teamed with Rough Guides and other concerned industry partners to support Climate Care, which allows people to offset the greenhouse gases they are responsible for with contributions to energy-saving projects and other climate-friendly initiatives in the developing world. Lonely Planet offsets all staff and author travel.

For more information, turn to the responsible travel pages on www.lonelyplanet .com. For details on offsetting your carbon emissions and a carbon calculator, go to www .climatecare.org.

GETTING INTO TOWN FROM SCHIPHOL AIRPORT

Train

Trains run to Amsterdam Centraal Station (Map pp38-9, E2) 24 hours a day; between 6am and midnight, they run at least every 15 minutes. The trip takes 20 minutes and costs €3.80. Ticket machines accept coins and credit cards with chips; ticket-office purchases add €0.50.

Bus

Connexion (☎ 038-339 47 41; www.airporthotelshuttle.nl; one-way/return €15/24/50) drops you at your hotel door. Departures are every 30 minutes from 6am to 9pm; look for the desk by Arrivals 4.

Taxi

A taxi to the city centre takes 20 to 30 minutes (longer in rush hour) and costs €40 to €45. Shared taxis start at €21, and must be booked ahead at www.schiphol.nl.

FERRY

From London, **Stena Line** (www.stena line.co.uk) runs a service that includes the ferry between Harwich and Hoek van Holland, plus connecting rail service on either end. Total travel time is 13 hours during the day and 12 hours for the night trip.

CAR

Public lots are located around the city, but it is more convenient to leave your car at a park-and-ride lot on the outskirts. The fee (€6 for 24 hours) includes public transport tickets. For more info see www.bereikbaaramsterdam.nl.

GETTING AROUND

Central Amsterdam is relatively compact and best seen on foot or by bicycle. The public transport system is a mix of tram, metro and bus, operated by the **Gemeente Vervoerbedrijf** (GVB; www.gvb.nl). Visitors will use only the trams, except in a few cases. This book notes the nearest tram/metro/bus stop after the 🚋 / Ⓜ / 🚌 icon in each listing.

The excellent website www .9292ov.nl calculates routes, costs and travel times. Enter your street address, and 'Amsterdam' in the Plaats line.

All public transport in the Netherlands is accessible via a pass card called the *OV-chipkaart*. Tram conductors and GVB vending machines sell one-hour cards (€2.60), but daylong or multiday travel passes (p174) can be better value. Refillable cards enable cheaper rides, charged by distance, but they make sense only for repeat or long-stay

DIRECTORY

RAIL EASY TRAVEL

Amsterdam has very convenient train connections with other European capitals. Budget airfares may look tempting, but given odd flight times, out-of-the-way airports and perhaps a taxi fare to the airport, the train is often much handier and occasionally even cheaper. High-speed tracks between Amsterdam and the Belgian border, installed in 2009, make the trip from southern points even more efficient. Consider extending your trip with an extra day in Brussels or Paris – as easy as hopping off and hopping back on.

visitors. They cost €7.50, and you must have at least €4 on the card at all times to ride city transport, and €20 to ride national trains.

Centraal Station, where most visitors arrive, is under long-term construction, making it a little difficult to find all the tram stops. For trams 4, 9, 16, 24 and 25 head to the left (east) when you come out the front of the station.

TRAVEL PASSES

The GVB offers passes in *OV-chipkaart* form for one to seven days (per 24/48/72/96/120/144/168 hours €7/11.50/15.50/19.50/23/26/29). They're available at VVV offices (p179), some hotels, metro-station machines (up to 72 hours only) and tram conductors (24 hours only). The All in 1 Travel

Ticket (per 24/48/72/96 hr €13.20/17.25/20.85/24.45) includes round-trip fare from Schiphol; get it at the Holland Tourism desk at the airport. The I amsterdam Card (p176) also includes a travel pass.

TRAM

Fast, frequent trams operate between 6am and 12.30am. On trams with conductors, enter at the rear; you can buy a single-ride *OV-chipkaart* (left) when you board. On trams without conductors (line 5, and some on line 24), buy a ticket from the driver. When you enter and exit, wave your card at the pink machine to 'check in' and 'check out'.

METRO & BUS

The metro and buses serve primarily outer districts; tourists rarely need these services. But the small Stop/Go bus can be useful: it runs from Waterlooplein (Map pp122-3, B4) to Oosterdok (Map pp134-5, A4) and the harbour via Prinsengracht between 9am and 5.30pm; flag it down, as there are no fixed stops.

NIGHT BUS

Nachtbussen (night buses) run after other transport stops, between 1am and 6am. The routes radiate out from Centraal Station, with service roughly every hour. Dedicated night-bus route maps and schedules are posted at the stops the buses serve.

FERRY
Free ferries run to Amsterdam-Noord, departing from piers behind Centraal Station. The ride to Buiksloterweg is the most direct (five minutes) and runs 24 hours. Another boat runs to NDSM-werf (15 minutes) between 7am and midnight (1am on Saturday), and another goes to IJplein (6.30am to midnight). Bicycles are permitted.

BICYCLE
Many visitors rent a bike towards the end of their stay and wish they had done so sooner. We can't recommend it highly enough. Rental companies can be found all over town; all require ID plus a cash deposit or credit-card imprint. Most have a variety of bicycles, starting with single-speed models with coaster brakes; handbrakes and gears cost a little more. Helmets are generally not available (the Dutch don't wear them), and theft insurance is typically optional – you shouldn't need it if you're careful about locking your bike correctly.

Handy to Centraal Station is **Holland Rent-a-Bike** (Map pp38-9, C4; ☎ 622 32 07; Damrak 247; per 24hr €15) in the Beurs van Berlage (p41). **Mike's Bike Tours** (Map pp82-3, C3; ☎ 622 79 70; www.mikesbiketoursamsterdam.com; Kerkstraat 134; per 24hr €10) rents low-slung cruisers that are good for biking novices. **Black-Bikes.com** (De Zwarte Fietsenplan; Map p38-9, B4; ☎ 670 85 31; www.black-bikes.com; Nieuwezijds Voorburgwal 146; per 24hr €15) rents cargo bikes and tandems for toting kids; rates include obligatory insurance.

For route planning, see www.routecraft.nl, which calculates best bike paths; for English, click on 'Bikeplanner' then the British flag.

TAXI
Metered taxi rates start at €7.50, which includes the first kilometre. The taxi industry in Amsterdam is a source of many complaints from tourists and locals. By far the most reliable service is **Taxicentrale Amsterdam** (TCA; ☎ 777 77 77). Non-TCA drivers sometimes cannot change large bills (or claim they can't) and often don't know smaller streets. You can also find taxis at stands at Centraal Station (Map pp38-9, E2), Leidseplein (Map pp82-3, A3) and a few hotels. At taxi stands look for a pink ID card displayed in the window, which allows drivers to drive on tram lines, and shows the driver has passed a city knowledge exam; you're not obliged to take the first car in the queue.

Tuk-tuks (per ride €3; ☿ 10pm-3am Fri & Sat mid-May–Oct) connect Rembrandtplein, Leidseplein and De Pijp. Fares for **bike taxis** (☎ 062 824 75 50; www.wielertaxi.nl) are €1 for three minutes, but drivers may negotiate.

to add. Click on 'Stadswandelingen' on the website for English info and online reservation page.

Agency **Like-A-Local** (www.like-a-local.com) helps arrange tours, home visits and meals with Amsterdammers. Get the inside scoop on art and architecture with tony **Artifex** (☎ 620 81 12; www.artifex-travel.nl, in Dutch), or more affordable **Urban Home & Garden Tours** (☎ 688 12 43; www.uhgt.nl; from €28.50). For a tour of Vermeer's work in the Rijksmuseum, contact art historian **Kees Kaldenbach** (☎ 669 81 19; www.johannes vermeer.info; €45). The Prostitution Information Centre (p43) covers lower-brow topics in De Wallen (the red-light district).

BIKE TOURS

AmsterBike (Map pp134-5, B3; ☎ 419 90 63; www.amsterbike.eu; Piet Heinkade 11a; from €17.50) runs a two-hour modern architecture tour, as well as more typical city and countryside tours.

BOAT TOURS

By far the best option is **St Nicolaas Boat Club** (Map pp82-3, A3; www.amsterdam boatclub.com) and its small, open boats that can go into the narrowest canals. The entertaining captains only ask for a donation at the end. Sign up at Boom Chicago (p92). The small **Canal Hopper** (Map pp38-9, D3; ☎ 535 33 03; www.canal.nl/hopper; €17) is a pale imitation, but at least it doesn't have polyglot tour-guide patter; look for a dock on the Damrak. The larger boats are all hopelessly stodgy; a one-hour tour with any company is about €13. A great way to see old industry and new architecture on the IJ is on a boat operated by the **Amsterdam Public Transport Museum** (☎ 423 11 00; www.museum-ijveren-amsterdam.nl, in Dutch; full/half tour €5/3; per bicycle €3). They run from pier 14 behind Centraal Station on Sundays only, from late March to late October; see the website for schedules.

TELEPHONE

The Netherlands uses GSM 900/1800 mobile (cell) phones, compatible with Europe and Australia but not with the North American GSM 1900 (some convertible phones work in both places). SIM cards start around €7.50.

Coin public phones have made a comeback, but many still take only cards, available at post offices, VVV and GWK offices, and tobacco shops for €5, €10 and €20.

COUNTRY & CITY CODES

The country code for the Netherlands is ☎ 31 and the Amsterdam area code is ☎ 020 (leave off the 0 when dialling from abroad). Mobile numbers (which cost more to call) start with ☎ 06. Free information numbers start with ☎ 0800; those beginning with ☎ 0900 cost between €0.10 and €1.30 per minute. Directory inquiries are on ☎ 0900 80 08.

To call internationally from Amsterdam, dial ☎ 00 before the country code; to reach an operator, dial ☎ 0800 04 10.

TIPPING

Tipping isn't compulsory, but 5% to 10% in taxis is common. In restaurants, round up the total to the nearest €1 or €5 – a 10% tip is considered very generous. Hand money directly to the server, saying the total that you want to pay: 'Make it €40', for example. Toilet attendants expect €0.25 to €0.50, or whatever's posted. Doormen at clubs get €1 or €2 on your way out.

TOURIST INFORMATION

The main tourist information source, the **VVV** (Netherlands Tourism Board; ☎ 0900 400 40 40; ☉ 9am-5pm Mon-Fri), is extremely helpful. It books hotel rooms and sells maps, discount passes and theatre tickets. Its information number is €0.40 a minute; from abroad call ☎ 020 551 25 25 (no extra charge). Offices, managed by the Amsterdam Tourism & Convention Board, include: **in front of Centraal Station** (Map pp38-9, E2; Stationsplein 10; ☉ hotel bookings 9am-5pm, transport & ticket information 7am-9pm Mon-Fri, 8am-9pm Sat & Sun); **inside Centraal Station** (Map pp38-9, E2; Platform 2a; ☉ 8am-7.45pm Mon-Sat, 9am-5pm Sun); and **Leidseplein** (Map pp82-3, B3;

Leidseplein 1; ☉ 9am-5pm Mon-Sat, 9am-5.15pm Sun). **Holland Tourist Information** (☉ 7am-10pm), also VVV-run, is at Schiphol airport.

TRAVELLERS WITH DISABILITIES

Travellers with reduced mobility will find Amsterdam only moderately equipped to meet their needs. Most offices, museums, metro stations and public buildings have lifts and/or ramps and accessible toilets catering for those with disabilities. But many budget and midrange hotels are in old buildings with steep stairs and no lifts, and cobblestone streets are rough for wheelchairs. Restaurants tend to be on ground floors, though 'ground' sometimes includes a few steps. People with a disability get discounts on public transport; tram lines 5 and 24 run wheelchair-accessible carriages, but at rush hour, trams can be crowded and difficult to board. All buses are accessible, as are metro stations. This book's listings include the ♿ icon only where both entrance and toilets are accessible. The Uitburo (boxed text, p93) and the VVV (left) can provide details regarding access to entertainment venues and museums. More questions? Check the accessibility guide at www.toegankelijkamsterdam.nl, and contact **Cliëntenbelang Amsterdam** (Handicap Geen Punt; ☎ 752 51 00), which maintains the site.

>INDEX

See also separate subindexes for See (p188), Shop (p189), Eat (p190), Drink (p191) and Play (p192).

◉ SEE

000 map pages

🍴 EAT

INDEX

000 map pages